First published by
Independent Thinking Press
Crown Buildings, Bancyfelin, Carmarthen, Wales, SA33 5ND, UK
www.independentthinkingpress.com
Independent Thinking Press is an imprint of Crown House Publishing Ltd.

British Library Cataloguing-in-Publication Data

A catalogue entry for this book is available from the British Library.

Print ISBN 978-1-78135-007-2
Mobi ISBN 978-1-78135-045-4
ePub ISBN 978-1-78135-046-1
ePDF ISBN 978-1-78135-047-8

Printed and bound in the UK by
Stephens and George, Dowlais, Merthyr Tydfil

This book is dedicated to my wife Jackie and our dear friend and colleague Kevin Robinson who died in November 2009. I hope Kevin's spirit lives on in this book and that he would have approved of the ideals it promotes.

Contents

Part I: Our World in the Twenty-First Century

Helping children to become responsible global citizens who will help to change the world for the better.

Part II: Creating Responsible Citizens in Our Schools and Communities

Promoting a sense of aspiration and ambition within learners and also providing ideas for how they can make a positive difference to the school and the locality.

Introduction

In a time of drastic change it is the learners who inherit the future.
The learned usually find themselves equipped to live in a world that no longer exists.

Eric Hoffer

I remember it like yesterday. It was my first ever interview for a deputy headship and I braced myself for the first question. It certainly wasn't what I expected: 'A hymn, a prayer and a telling off – is this an accurate description of a school assembly?' I can't remember how I answered but it certainly made me think, and over thirty years later I am still thinking about it.

If a school assembly lasts twenty minutes then a child spends 63 hours a year in assembly and that equates to over ten school days of six hours each. This means that during their primary school years a child will spend 443 hours or 70 days in assembly and possibly a further 316 hours or 52 days during the secondary years. This can be either time that is simply lost and forgotten or hours that can be used to make a difference – to create confident individuals and responsible, deep-thinking citizens for the future.

Growing up in the twenty-first century can seem very complex and there are many things that seriously worry young people – global warming, depleted natural resources and how we can all live together harmoniously in a rapidly changing world. The generation of children currently passing through our schools will be the ones to resolve these issues for us. This will be achieved partly through the skills and knowledge they gather and partly through the development of an emotional and spiritual intelligence that will enable them to become good citizens who do the right things at the right time. This is what I have aimed to do in this book. The materials are aimed predominantly at school leaders and teachers in Key Stages 2 and 3 (ages 7–14). The photographs and activities suggested can be used to enhance learning in classrooms.

Eric Hoffer's comment speaks of a time of 'drastic change', and the twenty-first century has already brought considerable change with certainly more to come. Therefore, the premise behind this book is that more than ever children need to be equipped to think deeply and make appropriate choices about what is right and wrong, good and evil, beautiful and ugly.

Many of the assemblies build from ideas in my previous book, *Inspirational Teachers Inspirational Learners* (2011). In turn, I hope the suggestions equip you to lead inspirational assemblies that pass the three generations test: the children remember them in the short term; they still remember them when they become parents; and finally they are able to tell their grandchildren about them.

The book is laid out in two parts:

■ Part I: Our World in the Twenty-First Century aims to help children to become responsible global citizens who will help to change the world for the better.

■ Part II: Creating Responsible Citizens in Our Schools and Communities aims to promote a sense of aspiration and ambition within learners and also provide ideas for how they can make a positive difference to the school and the locality.

The book also recognizes the pressures school leaders and teachers are under. Therefore the materials for each theme are presented in three ways:

- Three Star Assemblies ✪✪✪: These are for those moments when you think: 'Help, I've hardly any time to plan an assembly!' For these assemblies, you can simply pick up the book and read the story or account and follow the activities planned.

- Four Star Assemblies ✪✪✪✪: These are for the occasions when you've got a bit longer to prepare. They might involve groups of children, music or film footage. Many of the themes and resources provided open up opportunities for Philosophy for Children activities in the classroom. Sometimes these could be highly worthwhile learning activities that may not be incorporated into an assembly. On other occasions the children's thinking can enhance the assemblies. Sometimes the materials could lead to a follow-up assembly (which means that many of the assemblies develop into two assemblies).

- Five Star Assemblies ✪✪✪✪✪: These are for the occasions when you need the 'Rolls Royce' model of deep, rich and meaningful assemblies. Perhaps it is because Ofsted are about to

arrive. Again there are suggestions for how you can involve the children as described in the section above. On some occasions the Five Star Assembly can become a further follow-up assembly, and so on these occasions each assembly grows into three assemblies!

One of the concepts I have become increasingly interested in over recent years is the power of the six word story. Many of the world's largest and most successful businesses use six word stories as an advertising technique. Here are a couple of examples: 'Engineered to move the human spirit' (Mercedes Benz)' and 'We're number two. We try harder' (Avis Rent a Car).

Six words are deemed to be the smallest number of words you can use to write a complete story. Some of the assemblies and activities urge the children to use six really powerful words to describe an image or capture part of the assembly. The six word story can also be a brilliant method of introducing reflection at the end of the assembly.

Many of the assemblies are designed to incorporate a Team of Experts model. Often when you view a live factual programme on television you see a research team in the background working away on computers providing up-to-the-minute information. This approach is built into many of the assemblies. All you need to do is create a team of four or five experts who set out to find additional information relating to the assembly whilst it is taking place. This methodology increases pupil participation and also demonstrates the speed at which we can gain information, adding to the twenty-first century feel of the assembly. However, the group may need the guidance of an adult until it becomes an accepted part of the routine.

It should be stressed that the contents of this book and Jane Hewitt's stunning images on CD Rom are designed for wide useage. They have not just been produced with the school assembly in mind. The stories, articles and pictures can be used in a variety of ways by the teacher in his or her own classroom. As suggested, they can promote deep and rich activities within 'Philosophy for Children' or promote an area of research for a small group of pupils. This in turn could lead to high quality writing opportunities across a range of genres. Equally the ideas promoted could be used to introduce a class or group to those projects which have the big emotional hook, such as:

■ Is slavery confined to the past?

■ How can we live harmoniously in rapidly changing communities?

■ Why should we recycle?

■ Who are the real super heroes who have changed our community, or changed our country or changed our world?

Eric Hoffer is correct to tell us that we live in a time of drastic change. I hope that this book does help to create learners who inherit the future and help to make the world a better place, but I also hope that you enjoy exploring the themes with the children and young people in your care.

Part I
Our World in the Twenty-First Century

Helping children to become responsible global citizens
who will help to change the world for the better.

1.
The Bitter Taste of Chocolate

Three Star Assembly ★★★

Script

Take a look at this image. When you stand in front of the shelves in any shop or supermarket you will see items attractively displayed. They seem to say to you 'reach out and buy me'. The goods in front of you may have travelled thousands of miles and from all the continents of the world. However, many of the people involved in the production chain may live in poverty, working long hours for very little pay. They will not see shops with well-stacked shelves. In their shops the range of goods they may buy will be very limited and they will have just enough cash to buy the bare essentials. This story explores child labour in the chocolate industry.

During the assembly you could use a small Team of Experts with laptop or tablet computers to find out any additional information about child labour in the chocolate industry or the work of Fairtrade, which could then be shared later.

Story

Chris settled down on the sofa facing his 42-inch plasma television screen. He took another bite of his favourite chocolate bar and felt it melt in his mouth. He felt the sensation and the flavour exploding on his taste buds. Life was pretty good for this 12-year-old boy in the UK.

His chocolate bar had started its journey thousands of miles away in the hands of another 12-year-old boy, let's call him Wamah. In 2011 a BBC journalist visited the Ivory Coast in Africa and watched young children opening the cocoa pods that are used to make chocolate with extremely sharp tools called machetes.

The reporter commented:

During my visit to the Ivory Coast earlier this month it was easy to find child labour and difficult to see substantive measures to prevent it.

The sight of seeing young children carrying machetes and pesticide equipment is common throughout the cocoa belt.

More than 800,000 children there are believed to do some form of cocoa related work. I found a group walking along a muddy path towards trees where bright yellow cocoa pods hung ready for harvest.

Silently the children squatted down and started work. They wore torn and grubby shorts and T-shirts. There was no laughter or play.

On their legs were scars from machete injuries. There was no first aid kit around and no protective clothing.

One – a 12-year-old – said that his parents lived far away and he had not seen his family for three years.[1]

Life was pretty bad for this 12-year-old boy. He is very different from Chris comfortably settled in front of the television. This young boy has never tasted chocolate and most likely never will.

Shortly after this story was broadcast, the confectionary company concerned said they would start an enquiry into the use of child labour on the farms that supply them with cocoa. They also pointed out that this could mean they will have to pay much more for cocoa beans. Ten years earlier the giant food firm had signed a commitment to bring an end to child labour within the industry.

The chocolate industry makes billions of pounds in profit every year.

---

1 See www.bbc.co.uk/news/world-africa-15917164 (accessed 28 August 2012).

Questions to consider:

- Which items on the shelf look the most tempting and say 'come and buy me'?

- Would you change your mind if you knew that children had worked in unsafe conditions to make the product?

- How do you think a large confectionary company should spend some of its profits?

- Should the wrappers on chocolate bars indicate whether it has been produced using child labour?

- If we stopped buying chocolate would it help to bring about change?

- Can you sum up the messages in this assembly in just six powerful words?

If you have used the Team of Experts model you could ask then to provide additional information at this point.

Four Star Assembly ⭐⭐⭐⭐

With some preparation you can find many pictures of child labour on cocoa farms on the Internet. There are also many newspaper accounts which could be used to support your assembly.

Work with a group of children to explore the concept of Fairtrade chocolate, and see if it is possible to establish which chocolate producers guarantee that their confectionery has been manufactured without the use of child labour. It may also be possible to do a price comparison between Fairtrade chocolate bars and those that might have been produced using child labour. The children could present their information in the assembly through a PowerPoint presentation or they could make their own news broadcast using Flip Video.

The children could also write letters to the major chocolate producers urging them to cease using child labour.

Five Star Assembly ⭐⭐⭐⭐⭐

You could enhance the assembly further by using film footage relating to how child labour is used in the chocolate industry – many short films are available on the Internet. During the film the children could be asked to come up with some of their own questions. These could be identified during the assembly but used later in the classroom within a Philosophy for Children type of enquiry.

2.
From Sweatshop to High Street Shop

Three Star Assembly ★ ★ ★

During the assembly you could use a small Team of Experts with laptop or tablet computers to find out any additional information about the conditions in clothing sweatshops or sweatshop disasters. They could also find out which stores refuse to sell products made in sweatshops.

Script

Take a look at the image. There are three pairs of feet. One child stands in bare feet. The third child stands in a pair of training shoes that are starting to fall apart. These shoes cost so little to make and yet sell for so much. The children in the picture either can't afford them or can't afford to throw them away. This assembly explores the production of the training shoes and clothing which line the shelves of some of our shops. Imagine you are standing in your local sports shop. You have walked past the replica football shirts, the tracksuits, the bats and balls. Across the back wall is an array of training shoes. The advert above the display simply shows a famous athlete leaping through the air with three words written in bold letters underneath: 'Just do it'. The trainers come in a variety of colours and styles and might make you believe that even the most unfit person is capable of breaking a world record.

Away from the shop, however, there are many unknowns about the shoes. Questions such as:

- How much do the trainers cost to make?

- Where are they made?

- What are the conditions like for the workers who make them?

The big sports manufacturers say they have very strict codes of conduct for all the workers in their factories. They state that there are clear regulations about how long each person can work and that they must be paid a fair wage for the work they do. They also claim that their factories are closely monitored and that they would close them down if they broke their rigorous codes.

However, other people claim that this isn't the case and that a great deal of sportswear is produced in sweatshops in some of the world's poorest countries. A sweatshop is a place where the working conditions are considered to be dangerous or where people work excessively long hours, which makes them tired and vulnerable to accidents, or where the wages are very low. It has been claimed that an expensive pair of training shoes may actually cost just a few dollars to make. In May 2013 over 400 people were killed when the building used to house a sweatshop in Bangladesh collapsed. The building was unsafe with over 2,400 workers crammed into cramped spaces. Many of the goods being produced were heading towards high-street shops in the rich countries of Western Europe and the United States. There have been many other sweatshop disasters in other parts of the developing world.

Now imagine that we are a group of journalists and we want to find out the answer to the following question and report back our findings to a future assembly. The question is: Who is telling the truth?

Questions to consider:

- Look carefully at the image of the training shoe. How can you tell that it is old and nearly worn out?

- What adjectives would you use to describe the shoe?

- How do you feel about the fact that some children cannot afford shoes?

- Is it fair that in the twenty-first century some children have to walk in bare feet.

- Nike has a famous logo that says 'Just Do It'. What could they and other suppliers of trainers do to help children in poverty?

- What might you do next to find out more about how trainers are made?

- Who might you talk to?

- Who might you write to?

If you have used the Team of Experts model you could ask them to provide additional information at this point.

15

Four Star Assembly ⭐⭐⭐⭐

The assembly could get off to a more interesting start by showing some adverts from major sportswear manufacturers from television or magazines. If time allows, you could work with a group of children prior to the assembly to explore some of the issues surrounding sweatshops. There is a wealth of information and films about this issue on the Internet.

The children could draft letters to local sports shops or sportswear manufacturers and ask them about the conditions in which their goods are produced. If this was done well in advance of the assembly, any replies received could be included. Alternatively, you could tell the children in the assembly that letters have been sent and that the replies will be used in a later assembly.

Alternatively children could research the collapse of the sweatshop building in Dhaka, Bangladesh and share their findings in the assembly.

Five Star Assembly ⭐⭐⭐⭐⭐

Following the initial assembly, the children could carry out their own research into working conditions in developing countries. This could be presented as a newspaper account or a PowerPoint presentation, including film clips, in a follow-up assembly. Alternatively, they could produce their own news broadcast on Flip Video, which could be shared with the other children.

3.

Without the Man on the Plantation, the Man from the Supermarket Would Live in Poverty; With the Man from the Supermarket, the Man on the Plantation Lives in Poverty

Three Star Assembly ✪✪✪

Script

Take a look at the image. Another hard day's work has been done on the banana plantation. The worker sits at the side of an enormous pile of freshly harvested fruit. The bananas in the picture will sell for a considerable amount of money in shops and supermarkets. But where will this wealth go and how much will make its way back to the farm you are now looking at?

The following stories come from the Christian Aid website where further examples can be found. Ask the children to think about their reaction to these two stories – have they ever thought about what happens to their food before it arrives in our supermarkets? During the assembly you could use a small Team of Experts with laptop or tablet computers to find out any additional information about the work of Fairtrade.

Story

'My name is Maria and my father grows bananas in Ecuador. We all have to help because it is long and tiring work. Just as we were about to harvest them this year, the company from Europe who normally buy them pulled out because they found another farmer who would sell the bananas for less. This meant that the company in Europe could make more money. So now we have no money and lots of ripe bananas with no one to buy them. I don't know how we will have the money for food over the next few weeks.'

Story

'My name is Sam and my father grows coffee beans in Ethiopia. It is long and tiring work picking coffee beans, sorting them and drying them until they are ready to sell to people in the rich Western countries. Only a small amount of money paid for a cup of coffee goes to my father. The company that bought it from him keeps the rest. I can't go to school because all the family have to help with the coffee growing. The people who buy the coffee from us drive expensive cars, have nice houses and eat three times a day. We don't have any of those things.'

Bring into the assembly a bunch of bananas and explain to the children that you are going to demonstrate what happens to the money that we pay for the bananas in a shop. The assembly works well when you actually have 100 pennies and different children take on the roles outlined below:

- The man who owns the shop will receive 100 penny coins and will keep 32 of them.

- He gives 26 coins to the people who have helped to pack and transport the bananas from the ripening sheds and into the shop.

- He gives 19 coins to the people who ripen the bananas when they arrive in the country.

- He gives 13 coins to the people who moved the bananas from the plantation and then shipped them to the UK.

- Finally he gives just 10 coins to the person who worked so hard to grow them.

If time allows, repeat the process several times so that you can see how the piles of coins grow for each of the people. With each bunch of bananas purchased, the gap between the shop owner and the plantation grower gets wider and wider.

Questions to consider:

- Take a look at the image and decide how does the farmer look?

- What do you think it might be like to work on a banana plantation, and how might it compare to working in a supermarket?

- In the food chain activity that you have undertaken, who do you think the most important person is?

- Do you think that the money is distributed fairly?

- What do you think should happen next?

If you used the Team of Experts model you could now allow them to provide further information.

Four Star Assembly ✪✪✪✪

The assembly is made more realistic with the use of maps and photographs. A large map can be used to track the journey of the bananas from the plantation to the UK. You can point out the oceans crossed and also provide a timescale. There are also photographs readily available on the Internet of banana ripening sheds, packers at work, haulage lorries, supermarket shelves and so on.

The assembly could be made more meaningful by showing images of the homes and living conditions of those who live and work on plantations and comparing them to a typical family in the West.

Five Star Assembly ✪✪✪✪✪

You can extend the theme further by encouraging the children to look at the journeys of other key products such as cotton, coffee or chocolate. They could share this work through PowerPoint presentations or short films. The children could also consider what strategies they might employ to bring about change – for example, they could write to some of the largest retailers to express their concerns about working conditions in other countries.

There are many examples on the Internet of how the purchase of Fairtrade produce, including bananas, can greatly enhance the lives of the farmers on plantations. They show how when a fair price is received, and income is guaranteed, it can transform communities. New schools and roads have been built and the working patterns of workers change for the better. Children could explore the concept of Fairtrade and the impact it has had as a part of this work on bananas.

Themes: Child labour on tobacco farms,
how tobacco companies are destroying the rainforest
Timing: General

4.

How Many People Can
One Cigarette Damage?

Three Star Assembly ⭐⭐⭐

Script

How many people can be damaged by one cigarette? Is it one, one hundred, one thousand, one million or one billion? On 14 May 2011, *The Guardian* produced evidence to suggest that cigarettes, like the one in the image, could be threatening the life of young children thousands of miles away. As parts of the tropical rainforest are cut down to cultivate tobacco fields it affects each and every one of us. In other parts of the world the pesticides used damage wild life and the environment.

Trees: The World Bank Project (Tobacco Control in Developing Countries) tells us that much of the tobacco grown today comes from countries within the tropical rainforest. For every 300 cigarettes produced, one tree is cut down. This is because tobacco can't be grown on the same land year after year because it attracts parasites, which damage the crop. Forests are therefore regularly cut down to clear new land for tobacco plants. Trees are also burned in order to dry tobacco leaves. In the Philippines, 20,000 acres of forest are cut down every year from the rainforest so that tobacco can be grown. Some estimates suggest that one in twenty-five trees cut down in the world are used to produce tobacco products. In other countries the parasites, which blight the crop, are sprayed with dangerous pesticides, which affect the wild life as well as doing environmental damage. Let's examine some key facts.

Land: About six million hectares of farmland is devoted to growing tobacco worldwide. If the same land was used to grow food crops, it could feed up to 20 million people.

Child labour: The use of child labour on tobacco farms is not uncommon. In Malawi, about 80,000 children work on tobacco farms.

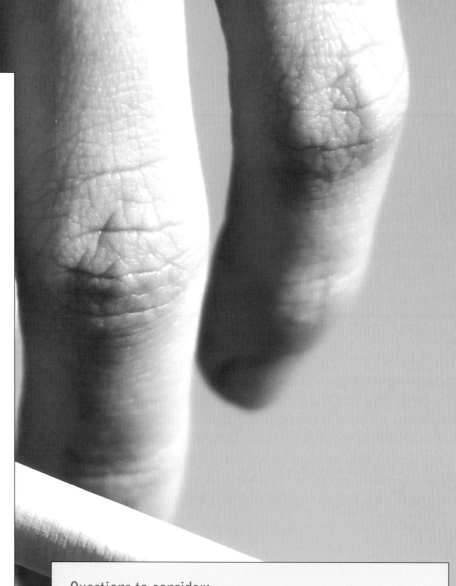

Story

A 5-year-old boy called Florala works every day on his parents' tobacco farm in Malawi. When asked when he would go to school, he shrugs his shoulders.

One thing is clear to Florala already: work comes first and education second. His sister, Ethel, is 12 years old but is only in Year 3. She only attends school sometimes because she has to work or because she is sick. 'I cough,' she says. 'I have chest pains and headaches. Sometimes it feels like you don't have enough breath.' This is because many of 80,000 child tobacco workers suffer from a disease called green tobacco sickness, or nicotine poisoning. Symptoms include severe headaches, abdominal cramps, muscle weakness, breathing difficulties, diarrhoea and vomiting, high blood pressure and fluctuations in heart rate, according to the World Health Organization.

When the children handle the tobacco leaves, it is done largely without protective clothing and workers absorb up to 54 milligrams of dissolved nicotine daily through their skin, which is equal to smoking fifty cigarettes. Farm owners routinely plead ignorance of the health implications. 'I never heard about touching tobacco leaves being dangerous,' says farmer Fraction Mkwantha, who plants 15 hectares of tobacco in Kasungu district in Malawi.[1]

---

1 See www.guardian.co.uk/global-development/2011/sep/14/malawi-child-labour-
tobacco-industry (accessed 28 August 2012).

Questions to consider:

- Take a look at the image and ask: who could be damaged by the person smoking the cigarette? How many other people could you add to the list?

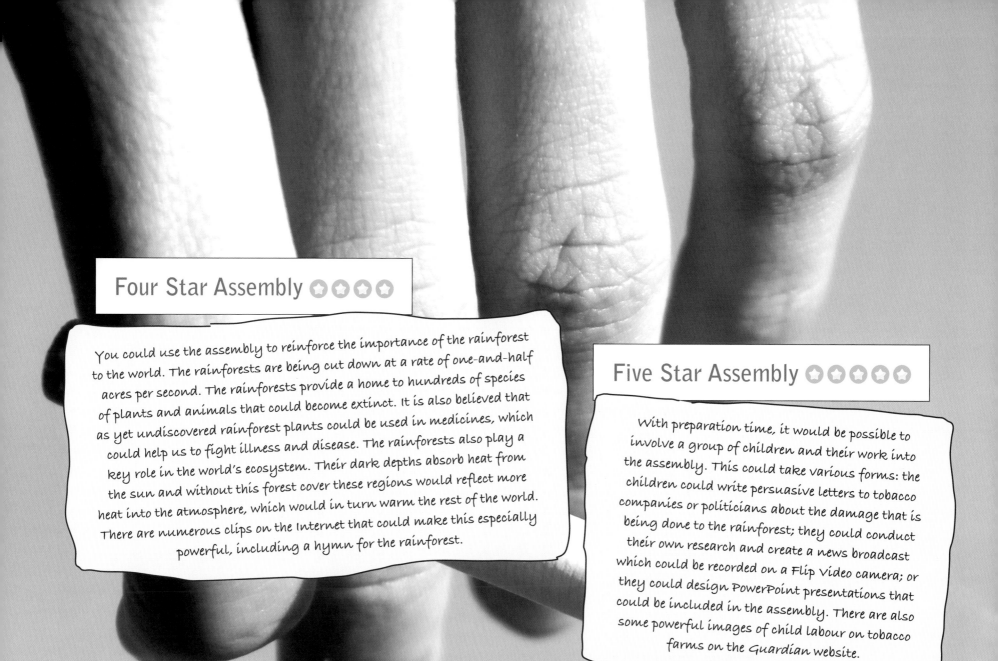

Four Star Assembly ✪✪✪✪

You could use the assembly to reinforce the importance of the rainforest to the world. The rainforests are being cut down at a rate of one-and-half acres per second. The rainforests provide a home to hundreds of species of plants and animals that could become extinct. It is also believed that as yet undiscovered rainforest plants could be used in medicines, which could help us to fight illness and disease. The rainforests also play a key role in the world's ecosystem. Their dark depths absorb heat from the sun and without this forest cover these regions would reflect more heat into the atmosphere, which would in turn warm the rest of the world. There are numerous clips on the Internet that could make this especially powerful, including a hymn for the rainforest.

Five Star Assembly ✪✪✪✪✪

With preparation time, it would be possible to involve a group of children and their work into the assembly. This could take various forms: the children could write persuasive letters to tobacco companies or politicians about the damage that is being done to the rainforest; they could conduct their own research and create a news broadcast which could be recorded on a Flip Video camera; or they could design PowerPoint presentations that could be included in the assembly. There are also some powerful images of child labour on tobacco farms on the *Guardian* website.

5.
Life in the Sixties ... the 2060s

Three Star Assembly ✪ ✪ ✪

Script

Take a look at the image of a crowded cityscape. Cities have changed so much over the last fifty years. Tall buildings reach for the skies. Tens of thousands of people now live and work within the buildings you now see. There will be many others who live there without a roof over their heads. What changes will we see in the next fifty years? This assembly takes us back to the 1960s and forwards to the 2060s.

Many see the 1960s as the greatest decade ever. They call it the Swinging Sixties. Man landed on the moon. Televisions appeared in homes in most countries around the world and car use became more common. If the 1960s were so superb, what will the 2060s be like? We are now over half way there and the changes have been rapid. The vinyl single has come and gone. The cassette tape has come and gone. Video recorders have come and gone. Take a look at the image. More and more people now live in our cities and they will continue to grow as more and more people migrate to them. In 2008, for the first time, half of the world's population lived in cities; by 2030 it will be 70%.

The following stories present two scenarios of what life could be like.

Story 1

It is 20 November 2069. Jake fastens the mask over his nose and mouth as he goes down from his apartment on the twenty-fourth floor and heads out into the smog-filled streets. Petrol prices have risen steeply in order to preserve the final oil reserves, which are now coming from miles below the mountain chains of Eastern Europe and the Arctic Circle, but it certainly hasn't reduced the numbers of cars on the roads. The air is so thick with fumes that everybody who ventures outside to walk even a short distance needs a mask, while others carry small machines that filter and clean the air they breathe. Those who can afford to, travel by personal helicopter, but it means that the noise is sometimes unbearable for those down in the streets. When copter-jams occur at peak times the noise is deafening.

After Jake has crossed the twelve lanes of traffic to the other side of the road, he walks past a new branch of Hip Savers. They are currently offering special deals on hip replacements, so if you have one hip replaced you get the second one done for half price. Jake had studied history when he was a child at virtual school. The lessons were wirelessly transmitted into his study zone – a small four metre square room – where he would work interactively with automatic teaching programmes. As a student of history, he knew that Hip Savers had grown from a chain of opticians from when people used to wear spectacles. He smiled at the thought – it was now much cheaper to have your eyeballs

replaced. It also reminded him that his parents would soon be going to have their extra memory implants fitted to their brains. This was a new treatment that followed research which showed that excessive watching of 3D television killed human brain cells, and this simple operation reversed the damage caused.

Jake thinks back to his virtual school days and remembers reading about the time when all children went to a 'real' school and spent time together every day. He thinks that it must have taken them ages to get there through all the traffic. He grins at the thought of sitting with other children all day long. Think of all the germs there must have been! No wonder pandemics were so prevalent in the 2020s.

Jake stops off to buy his breakfast pill. Since the population has risen to ten billion, everybody has to make sure that at least one meal a day comes in the form of a pill. He looks up at the giant computer screens to see how his favourite football team have performed in the World League. There are now twelve mega-professional football teams in the country and all had performed well. Each week their 250,000-seat stadiums were filled to capacity. On the edges of most large cities were older football grounds that were now disused. Many had been built in the 1990s and the early part of the twenty-first century. They had now become ideal locations for shanty towns. People erected simple lean-to buildings knowing that the old, desolate stands would provide shelter.

Families moved into the squatter settlements hoping to make a new life in the cities, but the reality was that crime and disease were prevalent in them. Other slums were appearing near to the huge landfill sites, which had to cope with ever increasing amounts of waste.

Today Jake was uneasy. He had to pass through some of the other ethnic sectors of the city and that made him nervous. Most people thought that it was preferable for different people to live in different sectors because they were better off mixing with their own kind. Perhaps terrorism had taught the world that was the case. Jake had to travel through different sectors on a regular basis, and he had always been perfectly safe. In fact, he was in more danger in his own sector as there were rumours that certain gangs of youths were carrying out taser attacks and stealing your identification chip.

While Jake feared that it could happen, he knew it probably wouldn't because he had always believed that most people in the world were honest and good. When he had studied history lessons during his virtual schooling, he had researched the lives of people like Martin Luther King, Gandhi and Nelson Mandela and had come to the conclusion that there was more in the world that united the different groups than separated them, and that if we understood each other more the world would be a better place.

Questions to consider:

- Take a look at the image: what words would you use to describe the scene? (Could you describe the cityscape in six words?)

- What do you think it would be like living in this city?

- Which bits of the city would be exciting, which would be dangerous?

- Where do you think the children play?

- If the story above became true, what would be the best bits of living in the 2060s?

- What would be the worst bits of living in the 2060s?

- What changes would you like to see made to prevent the worst bits in the story happening?

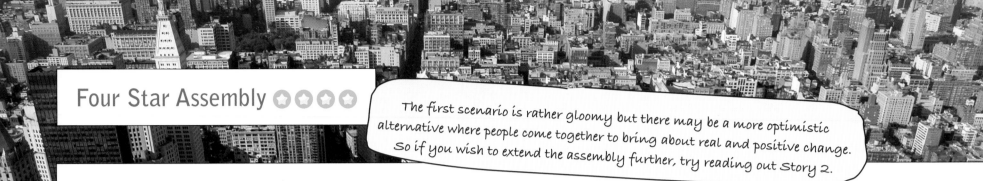

The first scenario is rather gloomy but there may be a more optimistic alternative where people come together to bring about real and positive change. So if you wish to extend the assembly further, try reading out Story 2.

Story 2

It is 20 November 2069 and Jake steps out into the autumn sunshine. The sensational 2060s are heading towards a close. This was going to be a day of great celebration as this decade had just been crowned the greatest in the history of the world. Just over ten years ago a historian had discovered a fusty, old document deep in the bowels of a government building. It had been written one hundred years previously on 20 November 1959.

The document was called 'The Convention on the Rights of the Child'. In it, all the nations had come together to agree that all the children in the world should be entitled to:

+ Equality, regardless of race, religion, nationality or sex.

+ Adequate nutrition, housing and medical services.

+ Special care if they suffered from any form of disability.

+ Love, understanding and protection.

+ Free education and places to play.

+ Relief at a time of a disaster.

+ Protection from neglect, cruelty and exploitation.

+ To be brought up in a world free from discrimination and within a spirit of peace and tolerance.

When it was discovered ten years previously, the world's greatest politicians had pored over the document and were forced to admit that not enough was being done. There was still widespread illness in some poorer countries, people were still dying of starvation and some children still did not get an education or were forced to work on plantations to provide cheap food for rich people.

The world leaders argued with each other and blamed each other for everything that had gone wrong. However, they also knew that the populace were growing angry with them. People were tired of the politicians' bickering and fighting and lies and broken promises while children continued dying through a lack of food, medicine and clean water. The people started to demand real change. They wanted all the world's nations to sign up to bringing real change on the one hundredth anniversary of 'The Rights of the Child'. They marched through the streets of the world's biggest cities with banners and placards until the world's leaders listened. Eventually they did and on 20 November 2059, one hundred years after its publication, they finally committed to bring about real change and signed their country's names to the new historical document, 'The Rights of the Child'.

And what a change the 2060s had brought! People from all races, faiths and cultures had come together to share and trust one another. A fair price was paid for food and goods. Child labour was brought to an end. All the children in the world went to school where they learned and played together. Everybody gained access to medicines and the Internet reached the most remote parts of the world so that everyone could communicate with and learn from one another.

The strange thing was that it didn't just affect the children. All the people in the world realized that there was more that united them than divided them, and that when they did unite, real change happened. People started living side by side in friendship. During the 2060s, the use of fossil fuels was greatly reduced and people readily shared their solar-powered cars. The climate stabilized and the threat of global warming was reduced. Ten years had passed and there had been no wars because all the energy had been put into bringing about equality. Crime rates had fallen and employment rates had risen.

Standing in the late autumn sunshine, Jake wanted to gain a good vantage point to see the procession as it passed – a procession which would celebrate the achievements of that marvellous decade they would always call the Sensational Sixties.

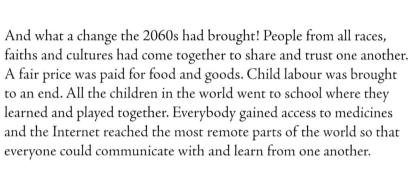

Five Star Assembly ⭐⭐⭐⭐⭐

You could ask a group of children to immerse themselves in both stories and imagine that they are Jake and living in the 2060s. From this viewpoint, they could hot-seat and answer questions put to them by other pupils. Alternatively, the children could prepare their own news broadcast, which could be performed or filmed and played during the assembly.

Another way of involving children would be to ask them to write their own contrasting stories of the 2060s – some optimistic and others pessimistic. The children could be encouraged to focus on issues like clothing, diet, transport, the environment, government, home and school life.

To add further interest you could start the assembly using images of the 1960s to show what an enormous period of change it was.

6.

One in Seven Billion: What Promise Would You Make to 6,999,999,999 People?

Three Star Assembly ⭐ ⭐ ⭐

During the assembly you could use a small Team of Experts with laptop or tablet computers to find out any additional information about the work of charities who work to improve water supply, sanitation or help communities to improve food supply.

Script

This image shows four children growing up in the twenty-first century. I wonder what the future has in store for them as the world's population continues to rise? It now stands at seven billion. It is possible to view population counters on the Internet and watch the population rise second by second. In some parts of the world there is not enough food or water. Sometimes there is insufficient access to medication and the idea of an education for children is merely a dream. There are other parts of the world where people live with plenty. The world can support a population of seven billion and more, but we all have to play our part. Vincent van Gogh once said, 'Great things are done by a series of small things brought together'. This assembly and the activities seek to capture that spirit. The photograph shows just four children – we will ask more about them later on.

It took thousands of years for the number of people in the world to reach one billion. The year was 1804.

It only took another 123 years for it to reach two billion. The year was 1927.

It only took a further 32 years for it to reach three billion. The year was 1959.

Fifteen years later it reached four billion. The year was 1974.

Another 13 years later the population reached five billion. The year was 1987.

The six billionth person was born 11 years later. The year was 1999.

Eleven years later on 31 October 2011 the seven billionth person was born.

So here is my first question:

You are just one person out of seven billion people. To give you an idea of just how many people this is, imagine counting out loud 1, 2, 3, 4 ,5, 6, and so on. How long do you think it would take for you to count to seven billion?

The answer is two hundred years. It would therefore take you two hundred years to count every person on the earth.

Now here comes my second question:

Do you think we should celebrate the birth of the world's seven billionth person or should we be worried?

The real answer is both. It is good news because some people are living longer. It is also welcome if every person could enjoy good health, live in a warm and safe house, be educated and earn sufficient money to live well and be supported in their old age. If we all work together this could be achieved.

However, many children in the developing world are born into poverty, especially in Africa. Some parts of the world don't have enough water to grow crops and the water that is available for washing and drinking is dirty and carries disease. In many countries there is inadequate sanitation. The world's oil reserves are becoming severely depleted and the use of fossil fuels is causing

global warming. Not every child is able to go to school and obtain an education. Various parts of the world don't have any electricity and the Internet and other sources of communication struggle to reach them. What could each of us do to help?

Here is my third question:

There are parts of the world where we need to build dams or convert land use to make sure we are growing as much food as possible. We need to find ways of reducing global warming which will mean finding alternative sources of energy. And we need to bring education to all parts of the world. What do you think we all need to do next?

> For this part of the assembly record the answers on a flip chart so the children see them being produced.

Here is my final question:

As one person in seven billion, do you think *you* can make a difference?

If the answer is yes, then which one promise would you make to the other 6,999,999,999 people in the world? However, as you make the promise, always remember that you will let down a lot of people if you don't keep it.

Questions to consider:

- Take another look at the image: what words would you use to describe the children or the place where they live?

- What things do you have in your life that these children may not possess?

- Do you think you own some things that they may never have heard of and could you begin to describe these things to the children?

- Do the children look happy and safe? What do you think helps children to feel this way?

- If you were allowed to say just six words to the world's politicians, what would they be?

> If you have used the Team of Experts model you can ask them to provide additional information at this stage.

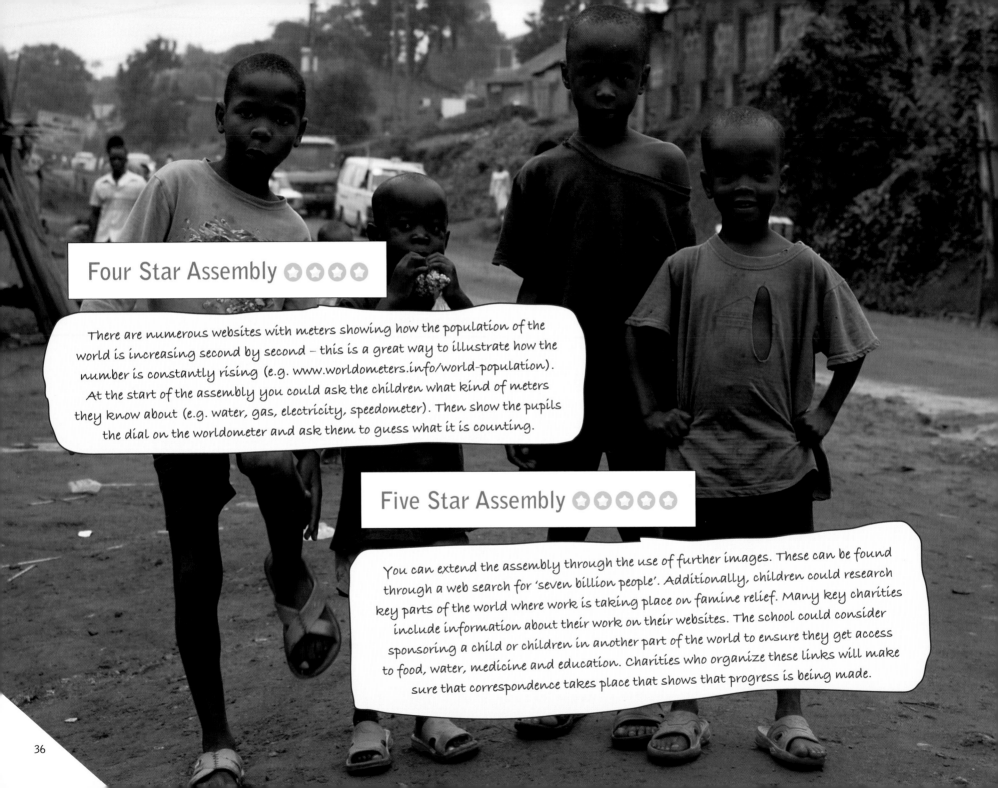

Four Star Assembly ★★★★

There are numerous websites with meters showing how the population of the world is increasing second by second – this is a great way to illustrate how the number is constantly rising (e.g. www.worldometers.info/world-population). At the start of the assembly you could ask the children what kind of meters they know about (e.g. water, gas, electricity, speedometer). Then show the pupils the dial on the worldometer and ask them to guess what it is counting.

Five Star Assembly ★★★★★

You can extend the assembly through the use of further images. These can be found through a web search for 'seven billion people'. Additionally, children could research key parts of the world where work is taking place on famine relief. Many key charities include information about their work on their websites. The school could consider sponsoring a child or children in another part of the world to ensure they get access to food, water, medicine and education. Charities who organize these links will make sure that correspondence takes place that shows that progress is being made.

7.

'There's a world outside your window, and it's a world of dread and fear'

During the assembly you could use a small Team of Experts with laptop or tablet computers to find any additional information about the work of Band Aid.

Three Star Assembly ⭐⭐⭐

Script

The title of this chapter comes from a famous pop song that has sold millions of copies. Look into the big eyes of the little girl. She looks like she wants something. I wonder what it is? Just maybe this song helped provide it.

Story

It was late October in 1984 and the pop star Bob Geldof sat down in front of his television to watch the news. One of the main stories was from famine-stricken Ethiopia. The film footage showed thousands of people starving and very close to death. He was so upset by what he saw that he knew he had to do something about it, and do it straight away. He wanted to prevent any more people dying. Over the next few days and weeks Bob Geldof set about this task. He hardly slept. He called his contacts in the world of pop music and somehow managed to convince them to clear a day in their busy diaries. They were asked to head to a recording studio in London because they were going to make a record. However, they were also told they would be paid nothing, either for their performance or from the sales of the record, because every single penny was going to be used to fight the famine in Africa. Bob Geldof refused to put down the phone until the musician at the other end of the line had said yes.

Eventually he had collected all the singers and musicians. However, there was still a major problem: at this stage there was no song to sing because it hadn't been written and no recording studio to make the record in because none of them seemed to be available. They needed to be booked much longer in advance.

Using the same art of persuasion, he managed to get his friend Midge Ure to help write the song and, after even more persuasion, eventually a recording studio was secured for the day. But the owners of the studio insisted that everything had to be completed on one day between the hours of 11 a.m. and 7 p.m. This

seemed unachievable. Different singers and musicians arrived at different times, which made rehearsals virtually impossible, but eventually each one had practised and recorded a small section of the song.

Somehow it all started to take shape and by the 7 p.m. deadline the super-group Band Aid had recorded their one and only record. It was called 'Do They Know It's Christmas?' The front cover of the record depicted families enjoying a traditional Christmas surrounded by gifts and festivities. In the foreground were two starving children clutching each other with fear and dread in their eyes.

Next, Bob Geldof started a tour of radio and television stations to promote the record. He urged people to rush out and buy it and try to stop any more deaths taking place. He made a promise that every penny raised would go to fight famine in Ethiopia. However, the then Prime Minister Margaret Thatcher tried to thwart Bob Geldof's ambition of using all the money raised to fight famine. She said they would have to pay tax on every record sold. This would drastically reduce the amount of money used to provide urgent food and medical supplies.

Bob Geldof prepared for his next battle. He had persuaded the musicians and singers to work for nothing. He had persuaded the recording studio to provide their services for nothing. He now prepared to take on the Prime Minister, who was often referred to as the 'Iron Lady', but when she made up her mind she always refused to change it. Well, perhaps I should have said that she *nearly always* refused to change it. On this occasion she did. This was partly because of the persuasive arguments made by Bob Geldof but also because the people of Britain had united behind him.

On 29 November the record was released and went straight to number one in the UK charts. It sold one million copies in the first week and 3.5 million copies within five weeks. Worldwide 11.8 million copies were sold. Since that time different versions of the record have been made using a range of pop stars. In 1985 Bob Geldof organized a huge concert to raise further funds called Live Aid. BBC reports indicate that as much as £150 million was raised by the recordings and concerts.

Bob Geldof had a considerable impact and today we celebrate what he achieved, but the battle goes on. Starvation still exists in parts of East Africa. In some areas a child dies from malnutrition every six minutes. This means that three children will have died from starvation during this assembly. The United Nations estimate that 870 million people, or one in eight people, suffer from chronic undernourishment worldwide. The same organization tells us that ten children die globally every minute as a result of malnutrition.

Questions to consider:

- What do you think the little girl is thinking?

- She looks like she wants something that is on the other side of the barbed wire – what do you think it might be?

If you have used the Team of Experts model you could ask them to provide additional information at this point.

Four Star Assembly ★★★★

It is possible to extend the assembly further by playing the music and/or video for 'Do They Know It's Christmas?' The video is available on the Internet and you can also find footage of the Live Aid concert. This can be really powerful in demonstrating to the children how people can unite to fight poverty and starvation.

Five Star Assembly ★★★★★

Many websites provide information about the current situation in East Africa, complete with case studies, which could be used to stress the reality of the current situation. Save the Children, Oxfam and Christian Aid regularly update their websites with the latest information, stories and accounts of how donations make a genuine difference.

8.
The Multi Million Dollar Plastic Red Nose

Three Star Assembly ⭐⭐⭐

BABY CLASS

Script

This image shows a class of children. I wonder how their classroom differs from a classroom in your school? Could a simple red plastic nose help to provide these children with a better classroom? Here is an assembly that could be used in alternate years around the time of Comic Relief. It tells the tale of how a simple red plastic nose generated over £600 million and transformed the life chances of children.

But let's first start with a quotation. A famous woman called Margaret Mead once said, 'Never doubt the capacity of a small group of people to change the world; indeed it is the only thing that ever has.' This is the story of how a group of people who normally make us laugh helped to change the world through Comic Relief.

During the assembly you could use a small Team of Experts with laptop or tablet computers to find out any additional information about the work of Comic Relief or find out about some of their success stories.

Story

First let us travel back in time to 1984 when the news broadcasts were filled with desperate scenes from Ethiopia where thousands of people were dying from starvation. Many people watched the scenes with tears in their eyes, shook their heads and simply said, 'Something has to be done!'

However, it was a group of comedians, led by Lenny Henry and scriptwriter Richard Curtis, who decided what should be done next. This bunch of much-loved comics who regularly made us laugh were about to tackle something far more serious. The challenge they took on was to improve the lives of poor and disadvantaged people in living in Africa. Comic Relief was finally launched live on Christmas Day in 1985 from a refugee camp in Sudan.

It started with a few concerts and live performances in theatres up and down the country with the proceeds donated to famine relief in Africa. Each time a successful event was organized, they sat down and said, 'But we need to do more!' And so they did, and the project grew and grew until a few years later, in 1998, Red Nose Day arrived on our television screens with an almighty bang.

In my case it was literally a bang. I had just finished taking an assembly when all of a sudden a parent in the hall put on a red nose and promptly smashed the world's second biggest custard pie into my face. Just as I recovered from that, and I was recovering my senses, the world's first biggest custard pie hit me full in the face. (Please replace this story with your own particular memories!)

The first Red Nose Day – including a television extravaganza, which was broadcast to millions of viewers – raised a staggering £15 million. Since that time, Red Nose Day has been held every second year and Comic Relief has raised more than £600 million towards good causes. Comic Relief introduced the concept of the 'Golden Pound' in which every penny from every pound raised goes towards the good cause, while the running costs come from other large organizations and businesses. Much good work has since been done. The Comic Relief website always contains a 'story of the month'. Here is just one of them:

> *Most children associate sand with fun on the beach or happy times in the sandpit. But for Basanta, age 12, and his younger brother Karma, sand is part of a gruelling day's work.*
>
> *Despite his young age, Basanta is a sand miner – which means he spends his days shovelling and filtering sand so it can be used for building materials. It's dusty, sweaty, back-breaking work – and can be extremely dangerous too. Recently, a mother and child were killed when a makeshift mine collapsed.*
>
> *Basanta and his brother are just two of the estimated 215 million children around the world who have to work to make ends meet. Without the extra cash he brings in, his family simply could not afford to eat. Unfortunately, they still don't have enough money to pay for Basanta to go to school.*
>
> *But thanks to the help of Kidasha, which is funded by Comic Relief, things are starting to change for Basanta. The project*

has provided him and his brother with a dedicated social worker who makes sure they know how to keep safe at work. She's also supporting their mother to cut down on the children's working hours, so they can get a vital education as well as having time out just to play. Basanta is now working less and studying more, giving him the chance to turn his life around so he can look forward to a much brighter and more secure future.[1] (You could replace this story with the current story of the month.)

Every time a Comic Relief event is held much of the money raised comes from children in schools and other organizations. They are helping young people like Basanta to be released from exhausting work in order to receive an education and improve the livelihood of their family. So when Margaret Mead said, 'Never doubt the capacity of a small group of people to change the world; indeed it is the only thing that ever has', maybe we should replace it with: 'Never doubt the capacity of a group of small people to change the world!'

---

1 See www.comicrelief.com/how-we-help/the-difference-we-have-made/personal-stories/basanta/ (accessed 28 August 2012).

Questions to consider:

- Take a look at the classroom in the picture – can you find any powerful words or sentences to describe it?

- Can you capture the spirit of the image in six powerful words?

- What do you think might be in your classroom that is not in this classroom?

- How would you describe the children in the photograph? Their surroundings may be basic, but do they look pleased and happy to be at school and enjoying their learning?

- What powerful words would you use to describe the life of Basanta in the story?

If you have used the Team of Experts model you could ask them to provide additional information at this point.

Four Star Assembly ⭐⭐⭐⭐

Red Nose Days have now been in existence for over twenty years. Many schools will have photographs of events that have taken place in previous years. These could be used to make a brilliant slideshow. While this could be prepared by you or another member of staff, it would lead to more powerful learning if it was organized by the children themselves.

If photographs aren't available, the children could write letters to former pupils in the area to ask them about their memories of past Red Nose Days or to ask to see any photographs they may have. Their stories could be read out or they could be invited in to tell their stories.

Five Star Assembly ⭐⭐⭐⭐⭐

You could extend the assembly further by providing an extreme contrast. You could start by looking at some of the comic antics of the comedians who set up Comic Relief (there is footage of Lenny Henry appearing on Tiswas, a Saturday morning children's programme from the 1970s, on the Internet) alongside a film of their work in Africa (also readily available on the Internet). There is also other powerful film footage of Comic Relief's work, for example: www.youtube.com/watch?v=AmiueJ6hy24/

9.
Can Sportsmen Succeed Where Politicians Fail?

Three Star Assembly ⭐⭐⭐

Script

Take a look at the picture of one of the world's greatest sportsmen. He is the kind of person who can transform a sports stadium into a cauldron of excitement and noise. Sportsmen can use their fame to do great deeds that help to improve our world. David Beckham, through his charitable foundation, has helped provide funds for wheelchairs for children who need them. He has raised awareness and helped to fight the spread of disease in Sierra Leone. In 2004, he was nominated to join the NSPCC's Hall of Fame for the work he had done to help safeguard children.

Let us now change sports and consider the story of a cricketer who helped to stamp out racism within his sport and possibly left a greater legacy than many governments.

Story

Conrad Hunte was born on the Caribbean Island of Barbados. His parents were poor and worked long hours on a sugar plantation. He was one of nine children growing up in a one-bedroom house. His parents believed that if he worked hard at school then Conrad would not live out his life in the same poverty. Each day he walked three miles to school and back again. His parents clearly hoped he would shine and do well in his studies, and he did shine. However, his success was not in the subjects on the school curriculum and nor did he achieve it behind his school desk. His success was with a cricket bat. He loved cricket and he practised hard and became very successful. He was watched by many scouts and coaches and was eventually picked to play for Barbados. He regarded this as a great honour. Some of the world's greatest cricketers had played for the island and he persevered to ensure he did well for them, and he did.

In 1956 Conrad Hunte's life changed direction. He left Barbados and sailed to the UK because he believed it would offer him new opportunities. He went to live in Lancashire. First of all he worked in a factory that built buses and later he worked in a cotton mill. At the time, there was a shortage of labour and Britain was desperate for workers who would undertake these jobs. The government actively encouraged people from the West Indies to move to the UK to work, sometimes even offering cheap transportation. However, when the immigrants arrived they often found life very difficult, and Conrad was no different. He experienced a lot of hatred and racist attitudes from some people.

Throughout this time Conrad continued to play cricket and he joined a local team in the Lancashire League where he continued to excel. Thousands of miles away, the West Indies Cricket Board were monitoring his progress and in 1963 they picked him for their international team. He quickly became a regular in the West Indies team and was a great success. He travelled the world playing cricket and scored hundreds of runs. He must have gone to some fabulous places but he also visited many places that made him feel sad. On his travels he saw people in poverty who were treated unfairly because of the colour of their skin, the language they spoke, the religion they followed or the place they had come from. He saw hatred and violence and this made him deeply unhappy.

In 1967, Conrad returned to England, where once again he saw black people being unfairly treated. This was a time when the country was heading towards race riots. He knew change was needed and he was totally opposed to any form of violent action. He did not want to see a single black or white person hurt. He knew that the only way forward was through developing respect, tolerance and understanding. He thought about giving up cricket to try and help this to happen but he knew that if he did he would have no money to live on.

Conrad Hunte tells the story of what happened in his autobiography, *Playing to Win*. He was walking through the streets one day thinking about his dilemma. He knew that he was a famous and talented cricketer who had scored centuries against every other country he had played. Some people thought he would become the captain of the West Indies, and at this time they were the best team in the world. However, he heard a voice in his head say, 'Look up and take courage. It is time to make a real difference!'

The next day, he resigned from international cricketing and set about his new work of encouraging people from all races to trust each other and live happily together. He moved to Atlanta, Georgia, where there was a great deal of tension between black and white people, but he worked to bring greater understanding between them. In 1991, he relocated to South Africa to help children in the black townships. As part of his work he developed the cricket skills of young black players while also working to build friendship and reconciliation between the country's black and white peoples.

The story of Sir Conrad Hunte poses many questions that are still relevant today.

Questions to consider:

- The image shows David Beckham – in what ways can a professional sportsperson be a good role model?

- When can a sportsperson be a bad role model?

- Do you think Conrad Hunte was right to give up cricket when he was so famous and successful?

- What qualities made Conrad Hunte such a good person?

- Conrad Hunte believed he could help create a better world – what actions do you think would make a difference to the world today?

- Which groups of people make up our local community today and how can we find out more about them?

- Are there still parts of our community where there is trouble and mistrust?

Four Star Assembly ✪ ✪ ✪ ✪

The children could research other sportspeople who have used their fame to make a difference to others. For example:

- David Beckham has supported a wide range of charities and causes as described in the introduction.

- The former cricketer Ian Botham has raised considerable funds that have allowed research into blood cancers – he has pledged that he won't stop this work until childhood leukaemia is beaten.

- The former Australian cricket captain, Steve Waugh, was a tough competitor, but when touring India in 1986 he was moved by children who were suffering from leprosy. Since this time he has been actively supporting victims of leprosy and their families through raising funds for the Udayan Home in Barrackpore, which removes disadvantaged children from deprived environments and provides them with education, healthcare and life opportunities.

- Footballer Didier Drogba has established a foundation to provide material and financial support for health and education in Africa, and he has joined forces with United Against Malaria (UAM) to fight the mosquito-borne disease which kills a child in Africa every minute.

- The tennis players Roger Federer and Andre Agassi work with disadvantaged and at-risk children respectively.

The children could research and write biographies of such people, not only to tell the story of their sporting success but also their good deeds and why they felt the need to make a difference. These could be shared in assembles or turned into a class publication. Typing 'sporting philanthropists' into a search engine will get you underway. The children could then go on to research other ways in which sport can bring people together.

Five Star Assembly ⭐⭐⭐⭐⭐

You could take the assembly further by telling the story of another famous cricketer called Basil D'Oliveira who played for England, even though he was born and grew up in South Africa.

Story

Basil D'Oliveira left his home country because there were no opportunities for non-white cricketers. At first he found it very difficult to adapt to life in the UK. He even asked where his changing room was because he didn't realize he was allowed to change in the same room as the white players. However, through hard work and determination he became successful and, after playing cricket for many years in England, he became eligible to play for the international team – which he did with great success. In 1968 he was picked for the England team that would tour South Africa. As a non-white player he thought he could help to change the attitudes of the apartheid government. He believed it was important that black and white people should be seen playing together.

However, his dream would never come to reality. The South African government said that Basil D'Oliveira was not an acceptable member of the touring team because he was black. As a result, the England team refused to play and the tour was cancelled. Sporting teams and sports people from around the world were shocked by South Africa's decision, and many of them refused to play either in South Africa or against South African teams. Other people who were not involved in sport decided to protest in other ways. Some people stopped buying South African goods in the shops and others joined marches and signed anti-apartheid petitions, placing immense pressure on the government to change their policies. Apartheid finally came to an end in South Africa in 1994 – lots of documentary footage is available on the Internet.

10.
The Boys Go To School and the Girls Collect Water

Three Star Assembly ⭐⭐⭐

Script

Take a look at this image of a little child by a family's water supply.

You could ask the children to look for signs of any pipe work that would allow the tank to fill and then to consider how long the water may last. Then ask the children to list all the different ways in which they use water on a regular basis, and record them on a flip chart. Some uses they may regard as essential (e.g. drinking, washing, and sanitation) and others for fun (e.g. swimming/paddling pools). After this, move on to tell the story of what the village of Bekere Washo in Ethiopia was like in 1999.

During the assembly you could use a small Team of Experts with laptop or tablet computers to find any additional information about the work of Wateraid or similar charities.

The Story of Bekere Washo 1999

Bekere Washo has no proper water supply. Water has to be collected from Amude Lake, which is 8 kilometres away, but even that is badly polluted and, as a result, many of the villagers suffer from diseases such as severe stomach cramps and diarrhoea. There are no hygienic and safe places to go the toilet. In parts of Ethiopia many children die before their fifth birthday because their young bodies are not strong enough to cope with the poor quality water they have to drink. The people live in poverty and have to work hard. There is no surplus money for medicine. Nobody is available to educate the people about the importance of clean water and sanitation.

Water collection is always the work of women who are helped by their daughters. The girls do not go to school as their brothers do. Shuma has lived in the village for six years and every morning between 4 and 5 o'clock she sets off to collect water. 'We have to go early,' she says, 'otherwise you cannot get good water, it would be mud.' The round trip takes five or six hours and carrying heavy containers of water is extremely tiring. On some days they make the trip twice. On alternate days they wash clothes in the river that feeds the lake.

Her friend is called Uma and she has four children, two boys and two girls. Her eldest daughter does not go to school – she stays at home to help with the water collection. Uma says that she needs someone to help her at home. 'Besides,' she adds, 'I don't think water collection needs a formal education.'

However, there is good quality water available in the area. Some of it is underground and would be easily accessible through systems of pipes. All that is needed are well-educated people who can find a way of doing this, but unfortunately too many of them don't go to school to get the education they need.

This story took place just over thirteen years ago and what the people of Bekere Washo didn't know was that help was around the corner that would transform the lives of the people in the village.

This is the story of Bekere Washo in 2012.

In 1999, a charity called WaterAid started to work with the villagers on a scheme to bring clean fresh water to the village. They used funds that had been donated by people like us. They had to make the money work hard, but a bucketful of pennies can soon become a bucketful of water, followed by another bucketful of water and then another. It was called the Gonde Iteya project. Many of the people in the village provided the hard construction work for the project while others took responsibility for its design.

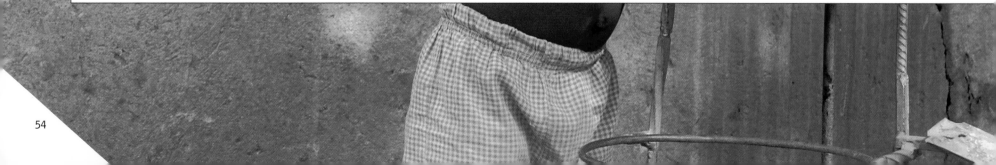

If you were to visit Bekere Washo today it would be hugely different. The community now has a clean water supply nearby and because the villagers don't have to spend time fetching water they can do other things. The women in the village spend more time helping their husbands to farm the land. Some of them are starting to run their own businesses selling goods they have made, and they are certainly more prepared to send their daughters to school. The arrival of the water supply is leading them away from poverty and is providing a better education for the young people.

The villagers no longer have to take their clothes to the rivers and lakes to wash them because they can now do it at home. They also have plenty of water for cooking, and bathing and washing their children. And the children are healthier than ever.[1]

The story of Bekere Washo is a marvellous success story and shows what can be done with commitment from individuals all over the world. Some of those people merely put a penny into a bucket. However, there are many other parts of the world where people still do not have access to good quality water or sanitation.

---

1 See http://www.wateraid.org/australia/what_we_do/where_we_work/ethiopia/ examples_of_our_work_in_ethiopia/default.asp (accessed 29 August 2012).

Questions to consider:

- How long do you think the water in the tank in the picture might last if it was in your home?

- How far might you be able to carry a bucket of water before putting it down?

- Can you provide a powerful six-word story that describes the village of Bekere Washo before and after the changes?

Let's go back to the list we started at the beginning of the assembly and put a tick by the things that, before 2012, the people in Bekere Washo might have used water for and a cross by those they would never use water for.

If you used the Team of Experts model you could ask them to provide additional information at this point.

Four Star Assembly

Prior to the assembly, or for an additional assembly, a group of children could investigate other regions of the world where the supply of clean water is a serious issue. They could also examine some of the key health statistics for these areas and create a presentation. The WaterAid website is a valuable source of information about the countries in which they work and provides key statistics about rates of population, infant mortality, child deaths under 5, life expectancy, availability of adequate fresh water supplies/sanitation, poverty and literacy levels.

Five Star Assembly ✪✪✪✪✪

How many pennies do you think can fit in a bucket? And if you did fill it with coins, would it weigh more than a bucket of water? Let the children have a go at estimating. You could take in one or more £1 bags of pennies to help the process along. Then try filling the bucket with pennies knowing that:

- 15 bags would buy the tools to dig and construct a well (and, yes, they could be used again).

- 90 bags would buy the cement needed for the well.

- 513 bags would pay for a drilled shallow well with a hand pump.

- 125 bags could set up a school health club.

- 3,750 bags could pay for a sanitation block in a school for 1,200 children.

11.
What Makes a Great Leader?

Three Star Assembly ⭐⭐⭐

Script

Some leaders, like Abraham Lincoln, have led their people to freedom, greatness and success. The image is of the Lincoln Memorial in Washington, DC. There is an inscription above the statue which says, 'Beneath these words, the 16th President of the United States sits immortalized in marble as an enduring symbol of unity, strength, and wisdom.' Abraham Lincoln fought for all those people in slavery to become free citizens. Other leaders have caused death, destruction and misery. In this assembly we will explore what makes a good leader and what we can learn from some great leaders of the past.

During the assembly you could use a small Team of Experts with laptop or tablet computers to find the names of some of the greatest leaders and a little about what they achieved.

Start the assembly by asking the children when we need leaders and also what kind of leaders we require in our schools, communities, country and world. You could draw up a list of the different leaders the children know about. Then extend the conversation to consider the questions: What makes a good leader? and what makes a bad leader?

Now write up a list of the features of good leaders and bad leaders as suggested by the children on a flip chart. Some examples are included below.

Good leaders
Listen to the people around them
Make difficult decisions
Plan carefully before taking actions
Loyal

Bad leaders
Make decisions on their own
Shout a lot
Fail to build friendships
Expect others to do the work

Story

Some people believe that the greatest leader of all time was born over two thousand years ago in a small village in China. His name was Confucius. He was born into a very poor family and was unable to attend school, but through perseverance and dedication he taught himself to read and write. Then he went on to study all kinds of things. He also spent a lot of time looking around him at what was happening in the world. The people around him also watched Confucius and realized he was developing great wisdom from his studies and observations. Confucius even seemed to know what to do when nobody else knew! As a result of his wisdom he began to develop the skills of leadership.

Confucius was very interested in leadership and he spent much of his time studying what good leaders did. He became governor of a town and later the minister of Lu state. When he was asked what kind of leader he would be he replied:

> Good leaders should use their eyes so that they may observe, their ears so they may learn, their face to reflect kindness, their manners to show respect for people, their words so that they may be truthful, and their dealings with other people to show that they are fair. They also know that kindness is a great virtue but that may not always provide the answer to a problem. They also know that bravery is a virtue but must not lead to rash actions when caution is needed. They know when to act quickly, when to act slowly and when to do nothing at all.

Confucius also believed that one of the main purposes of leadership was to allow people to live together in a peaceful and harmonious way. When he was asked how this could be achieved he replied: 'Do not do to others what you do not want done to yourself.'

Questions to consider:

- If 'do not do to others what you do not want done to yourself' was to become the way in which we all lived today, then what kind of things would always happen and what kind of things would never happen again?

- The Lincoln Memorial represents a leader who provided unity, strength and wisdom. What do we understand by these words and can we think of occasions when we have had to demonstrate these qualities?

- If you could describe the qualities a great leader has in just six powerful words, what would they be?

If you have used the Team of Experts model you could ask them to provide additional information about great leaders at this point.

IN THIS TEMPLE
AS IN THE HEARTS OF THE PEOPLE
FOR WHOM HE SAVED THE UNION
THE MEMORY OF ABRAHAM LINCOLN
IS ENSHR[I]NED FOREVER

Four Star Assembly ✪ ✪ ✪ ✪

Script

Here are three famous quotes from Abraham Lincoln that are in line with Confucius's thoughts:

'Whatever you are be a good one.'

'Do I not destroy my enemies when I make them my friends?'

'Those who deny freedom to others do not deserve it themselves.'

We will focus on the last quote. Before 22 September 1863, huge numbers of black people in the southern states of the United States were slaves. The website 'History of America' (http://www.ushistory.org/us/6d.asp) tells us much about the conditions under which the slaves lived. Slaves were not considered to be people; they were considered as property and were owned by others who could more or less do anything they wanted with them. Furthermore, because they were the property of others, they were required to carry their papers with them at all times so others would know which masters owned them. When the slaves were bought and sold, they were usually separated from their families. Slaves were forced to work for long gruelling hours in sweltering heat on plantations. It was considered illegal to teach a slave to read or write. Often the children of slaves were not even given a

name. In the state of Louisiana, it was considered appropriate that one slave per plantation should be whipped every four or five days. If a slave tried to escape, they were hunted down by dogs that were allowed to mutilate or even kill the slave.

Abraham Lincoln despised slavery. He considered it to be evil. Even before he became president, he spoke out against it and regularly received death threats. He wrote: 'In 1841, I had a tedious low-water trip, on a Steam Boat from Louisville to St. Louis. I remember that from Louisville to the mouth of the Ohio there were, on board, ten or a dozen slaves, shackled together with irons. That sight was a continual torment to me; and I see something like it every time I touch the Ohio, or any other slave-border.' However Abraham Lincoln did not waver. He fought long, hard and dangerous battles and eventually, twenty-two years after he had been on that steamboat, things started to change. He had fought for something he truly believed in and on 22 September 1863, laws were passed that would start to allow slaves to become free people.

There are many great leaders who used Confucius' principles. There are stories about some of them in this book and you could follow up the assembly with one of these. However, if you would like another story, then try this one about Abu Walid.

Story

A long time ago, in the eleventh century, invaders from North Africa attacked Spain. These people were called Moors. They were followers of the Islamic faith and brought many of their traditions to Spain. For example, they built many fine houses and mosques where people could worship. The Christians in Spain did not like what was going on in their country and built up their armies so that they could overthrow the Moors.

In 1085 a battle was fought in the city of Toledo and the Moors were defeated. Once more a Spanish Christian king ruled over the city. This was Alfonso VI of Castile, and he was a very wise man who knew that he had a duty to create peace. Alfonso made a promise to the leader of the Moors, Abu Walid, that no damage would be done to the mosque because it was a holy building and that the Muslim people would still be able to worship there.

One day Alfonso had to leave Toledo to visit other parts of the country. Before he departed he left strict instructions that the mosque was to be protected and that any Muslim who wanted to worship there must be allowed to do so. However, one of the archbishops threw out this ruling and when Alfonso returned he found soldiers had seized the mosque and were preventing people from entering. He was angry that someone had overruled him and the bishop was sentenced to death.

Abu Walid heard of this news and you might have expected him to be very pleased. He could have seen it as an act of revenge, but he didn't because he was also a peaceful man. Abu Walid pleaded with the king to save the life of the bishop because he too thought that the two faith groups could live harmoniously together. Alfonso was very impressed by Abu Walid's request and a pardon was granted.

Several years later a beautiful cathedral was built in the city. It was a truly fabulous building where the followers of Christianity would come and worship. As you enter the cathedral you can still see the statues of many Christian saints. But if you look very closely you will also see an effigy of a follower of the Islamic faith – Abu Walid, the strong, kind-hearted and forgiving leader of the Moors who wanted people to live together in peace and harmony.

Five Star Assembly ⭐⭐⭐⭐⭐

Too often leaders make up rules about the things people mustn't do rather than set out how they should behave if they are to be responsible citizens. Perhaps the children could think about their own school or class: if we want everybody to achieve, to feel they have a duty to achieve and help others to achieve, then what kinds of things must always happen?

12.

'Never again shall it be that this beautiful land will again experience the oppression of one by another'

Three Star Assembly ⭐ ⭐ ⭐

During the assembly you could use a small Teacm of Experts with laptop or tablet computers to find additional information about the work of Nelson Mandela in South Africa.

Script

Take a look at the photograph which shows a small boy. Especially look at his eyes. I wonder if you can see an element of fear. Then imagine a country where for centuries white people have ruled the land. They own the money and the wealth and live in fine houses. They are allowed to vote and choose their government. The white people look after themselves. In the same country, the black people live in poverty in poor housing. They are not allowed a reasonable education or proper access to medicine. Their wages are poor. They are not allowed to vote. If they try to protest to get equal rights they are often beaten, thrown into prison or shot. The white people oppress them.

It sounds difficult to believe that such a country could exist, but it did. This is the story of how one man and the people around him helped to bring real change to South Africa.

Story

Nelson Mandela was born in South Africa at a time when the majority of the people were disadvantaged by the colour of their skin. The whites owned most of the money and held power. The black people lived in appalling housing conditions with little space and poor sanitation. The black people were not allowed to vote.

Nelson Mandela campaigned hard to win freedom for black people and he joined an organization called the ANC or African Congress Party. They believed that their members should not obey laws that they thought were unjust, and they especially campaigned for free and compulsory education for all children regardless of their colour. As a result of his campaigning, Nelson Mandela was regularly sent to prison, but each time he came out he started to fight for equality all over again.

At one stage he proposed that if black people were not allowed to vote there should be a general strike. In a defence statement at his trial in 1964 he said: 'I have fought against white domination, and I have fought against black domination. I have cherished the ideal of a democratic and free society in which all persons will live together in harmony with equal opportunities. It is an ideal, which I hope to live for, and to see realized. But my lord, if needs be, it is an ideal for which I am prepared to die.' He made the declaration because he believed that violence might be necessary in order to bring change.

Shortly afterwards, Nelson Mandela was sent to prison once again, and this time it was for life. He was imprisoned in one of the harshest prisons in the world: Robben Island. He was sentenced to hard labour and spent long hours in quarries breaking up stone. He remained here for the next eighteen years.

However, the rest of the world was looking at South Africa very closely, and many were deeply shocked. They saw television footage of the appalling conditions in which black people lived and saw evidence of police brutality. Sports teams protested by not playing against South African teams and some people refused to buy South African goods. A huge pop concert was organized in 1988 to celebrate Nelson Mandela's seventieth birthday and to campaign for his release from prison.

The pressure for change slowly worked and eventually, after twenty-eight years, Nelson Mandela was released and South Africa agreed to end apartheid and to hold elections where everybody was allowed to vote as equals. Nelson Mandela was elected the South African President in 1994. Many white people thought he would seek revenge; but they needn't have worried. On the day he became the leader of the country he said, 'Never, never and never again shall it be that this beautiful land will again experience the oppression of one by another.' Nelson Mandela worked to bring peace, friendship and trust to all the people of South Africa and was awarded the Nobel Peace Prize in 1993.

Questions to consider:

- Take another look at the photograph – what might the boy be frightened of?

- Is it fair that people should be judged by the colour of their skin?

- What words would you use to describe Nelson Mandela?

If you used the Team of Experts model you could ask them to provide additional information at this point.

Four Star Assembly ⭐⭐⭐⭐

There are many images available of the black townships, which could be used at the start of the assembly. This will provide clarity about the living conditions that oppressed black people had to endure.

You could also use music that was written and performed as part of the campaign to bring an end to apartheid in South Africa. This includes Eddie Grant's 'Gimme Hope, Jo'anna' (Jo'anna refers to Johannesburg) and 'Free Nelson Mandela' by The Specials. There are numerous film clips from Nelson Mandela's seventieth birthday concert in 1988 on the Internet.

The 1999 film Invictus (directed by Clint Eastwood) contains many scenes of Nelson Mandela's first days as President of South Africa and they could also be shared in the assembly. Again, there are several clips available on the Internet.

Five Star Assembly ✪✪✪✪✪

You could begin the assembly, or extend it, by reading Carolyn Askar's famous story 'The Rainbow People'. It tells the story of how, although the peoples of the world have much in common, they can sometimes mistrust each other, but also how they can all come together, look after each other and make the world a better place. The story is published with Carolyn Asker's kind permission and you can find information at www.carolynasker.com.

Story (The Rainbow People)

In the beginning the world was very still and quiet. The ground seemed to be covered with dull-coloured rocks and stones. But, if you took a closer look you could see that they were not stones, but were tiny little people who were not moving at all.

One day a wind blew over the land. It warmed the people and filled them with life and with love. They began to move … to look at each other … to touch each other … to speak to each other … to care about each other.

As they explored their world they found coloured ribbons lying on the ground. They were excited and ran about collecting them up. Some chose blue, some red, some green, and some yellow. They enjoyed tying the ribbons around each other and laughing at the bright colours.

Suddenly another wind blew. This time it made them shiver with cold. They looked at each other, realized they were different … and stopped trusting each other.

The reds gathered and ran into a corner.

The blues gathered and ran into a corner.

The greens gathered and ran into a corner.

The yellows gathered and ran into a corner.

They forgot that they had been friends and had cared for each other. The other colours just seemed different and strange. They built walls to separate themselves and keep the others out. But they found that:

The reds had water but no food.

The blues had food but no water.

The greens had twigs to make fire but no shelter.

The yellows had shelter but nothing to keep them warm.

Suddenly a stranger appeared and stood in the centre of the land. He looked at the people and the walls separating them in amazement, and said loudly, 'Come out everybody. What are you afraid of? Let's talk to each other.'

The people peeped out at him and slowly some came out of their corners into the centre. The stranger said, 'Now, just tell one another what you have got to give and what you need to be given.'

The blues said, 'We have plenty of food to give but no water.'

The reds said, 'We have plenty of water to give but we have no food.'

The greens said, 'We have plenty of wood for a fire but we need shelter.'

The yellows said, 'We have plenty of shelter but we need warmth.'

The stranger said, 'Why don't you put together what you have and share it? Then you can all have enough to eat, drink, keep warm and have shelter.'

They talked and the feeling of love returned. They remembered that they had been friends. They knocked down the walls and welcomed each other as old friends. When they realized that the colours had divided them they wanted to throw them away. But they knew they would miss the richness of the bright colours. So, instead, they mixed the colours to make a beautiful ribbon. They called themselves the Rainbow People. The rainbow ribbon became their symbol of peace.

13.

How Did We Get the First African-American President of the United States?

Three Star Assembly ✪✪✪

During the assembly you could use a small Team of Experts with laptop or tablet computers to find additional information about Rosa Parks and the Montgomery Bus Strike.

Script

This image shows the White House, which has been home to the President of the United States of America since 1800. On 20 January 2009, Barack Obama formally became President of the United States of America. This was a great moment in history and news broadcasts all over the world were extended. The reason this was such a historic day was because he was to become the first African-American President. Just sixty-five years earlier this would have seemed impossible. In many US states, black and white people were required to live very separate lives. They went to different schools, restaurants and hotels. Virtually all public services were segregated. In the streets even the drinking fountains were labelled 'whites only' and 'coloreds only'. The laws required segregation. Black people were not seen as equal to white people.

So let us go to a day way back on 1 December 1955 when an extraordinary event happened. Most of the world was unaware that what occurred on this day would trigger a chain of events that would eventually enable Barack Obama to become President.

Story

A brave woman called Rosa Parks once said, 'I have learned over the years that when one's mind is made up, this diminishes fear; knowing what must be done does away with fear'. This is how she did away with her own sense of fear and helped to change a nation.

Rosa Parks got on a bus in the city of Montgomery after a hard day's work. The black people were required to sit towards the back of the bus and Rosa Parks sat on the front row of seats set aside for black people. A sign indicated where this row was. As more white people got on the bus, the sign was moved further back and Rosa Parks was told to give up her seat to a white passenger. This was standard practice on Montgomery's buses. However, Rosa Parks refused to move and give up her seat. The police were called and Rosa Parks was taken off the bus and arrested.

The minister at Rosa Parks's local church was called Martin Luther King. When he heard the news about Rosa Parks he urged African Americans to stop using the buses and so for the next 381 days they either walked to and from work or they found alternative ways of travelling. This was called the Montgomery Bus Boycott. The loss of money meant that the bus company was facing financial ruin and eventually they had to give in. A sense of justice prevailed and the bus company had to let black people sit wherever they wished.

However, the story doesn't stop there because Martin Luther King carried on this civil rights work. Throughout the late 1950s and 1960s, Martin Luther King spoke out and campaigned for black and white people to live together with equal rights. He always urged his followers to protest peacefully and he never supported violence, even though he was frequently attacked and his home fire-bombed.

His most famous speech, 'I Have a Dream', was delivered on 28 August 1963. It was later voted the greatest speech of the century. He spoke to over 250,000 civil rights supporters at the Lincoln Memorial in Washington, DC and told them of his dreams for the future, when he hoped 'the sons of former slaves and the sons of former slave owners will be able to sit together at the table of brotherhood' and that his 'four little children will one day live in a nation where they will not be judged by the colour of their skin but by the content of their character'.

While many groups and individuals were still were in favour of segregation, civil rights campaigners like Martin Luther King were having a real influence. The United States was changing and laws started to be made that guaranteed equal rights for all, regardless of their colour. Further changes followed and the laws slowly guaranteed equality for all. However, I still wonder if Rosa Parks had not sat on that seat, and if Martin Luther King had not delivered that speech, whether Barack Obama would have become the first African-American President of the United States.

Martin Luther King probably dreamed of the day when he would see a black president who was voted for by both black and white people together. He didn't live to see the changes he had dreamed of because he was shot on 4 April 1968. However, his work is remembered on the third Monday of January in the United States, which is now called Martin Luther King Day. Rosa Parks continued to fight for equal civil rights until she died in October 2005.

Questions to consider:

- Was Rosa Parks right to break the law on that December day in 1955, which paved the way for so much change in the United States?

- If Rosa Parks were to visit the White House now, what do you think the President would say to her?

Four Star Assembly ★★★★

The Internet contains many photographs related to segregation in the United States. It is relatively easy to find pictures of drinking fountains or restaurant doors labelled 'whites only' and 'coloreds only'. Photographs of Rosa Parks and images relating to the Montgomery Bus Boycott are also readily available. All of these images will help to bring the assembly to life.

Five Star Assembly ★★★★★

The transcript of Martin Luther King's speech and film footage of him delivering it are available on the Internet. A short section could be used to allow the children to see the power of Martin Luther King's oratory and how it started move the United States forward in its thinking.

14.
The Nobel Peace Prize

Three Star Assembly ⭐ ⭐ ⭐

During the assembly you could use a small Team of Experts with laptop or tablet computers to find additional information about Alfred Nobel and why he founded the Peace Prize.

Script

Take a look at the image of a pair of hands and think about the great deeds they could do. Then, think of an awful deed that they could carry out. Think about the scientist who is about to find a remarkable cure for an illness, the brave passer-by who finds herself helping somebody in distress or the surgeon who saves somebody's life. Each and every one of us is capable of great deeds which have the potential to make a difference to other people. Sometimes we may just make a difference to one person or to a small group of people, and sometimes we may affect many people. Equally, each and every one of us is capable of deeds which will hurt other people and cause harm.

This is the story of a man who thought he had done a great deed but later realized he may have done a great deal of damage, and what he tried to do next.

Story

Alfred Nobel was born in Sweden in 1833. His father was an engineer who built roads and bridges. Alfred had watched his father's work and was keen to make this very difficult and dangerous work easier. He became interested in finding a way of using explosives to clear the way for roads and also to make coal mining easier. He worked, studied and experimented and, in 1866, he invented dynamite, which is made from nitro-glycerine. It was an instant success and was quickly used to clear the land for big building projects. The construction of roads and railways suddenly became much easier, faster and cheaper. Alfred Nobel had made a considerable contribution to the world of engineering. He was not content with his invention, however, and he continued to improve the efficiency of his product. In 1876, he introduced a new explosive called gelignite.

Alfred Nobel took out patents on his inventions which meant that nobody could copy them without his permission or paying him money. His inventions made Alfred a very rich man and his explosives were in demand all over the world because they made such a positive difference to the world of engineering and mining.

However, dark clouds were gathering. Some people saw the advantage of using these explosives to make weapons for warfare, which could bring death and injury on a wide scale. The weapons made Alfred Nobel even richer but he was also becoming very discontented, because at heart he was a peaceful man and he didn't like his inventions being used for weaponry. As he grew older he became determined to use his money to leave behind a peaceful legacy that would make the world a better place.

Alfred Nobel arranged that after he died the money he left behind would be used to fund prizes each year for people who had helped others in the world. He decided to give prizes for literature, medicine, physics and chemistry, but most importantly of all, he decided to give an award to the person or organization that did the most to bring an end to wars and fighting or bring about peaceful solutions to the world's problems. This was to be called the Nobel Peace Prize.

There have been many famous winners of the award including Martin Luther King, who worked hard to bring about equal rights in the United States of America, and Archbishop Desmond Tutu, who did similar work in South Africa. Mother Theresa of Calcutta also won the award for her charitable work in India.

The prize is awarded on 10 December each year, which is the anniversary of Alfred Nobel's death.

Questions to consider:

- Think of a pair of hands. Can you identify five really good things that a person could make or good deeds they could do, and then five really terrible things they could make or do?

- Can you describe the powers that a pair of hands possess in just six meaningful but exciting words?

- Can you think of recent news stories in which there are examples of people who have made the right choices and performed good deeds, or the wrong choices which have led to bad deeds? (You may also be able to think of examples from a history lesson.)

If you used the Team of Experts model you could ask them to provide additional information about Alfred Nobel's Peace Prize.

Four Star Assembly ✪✪✪✪

To make the assembly more realistic you could incorporate newspaper accounts about major wars or conflicts currently taking place and where explosives are leading to destruction, death and injury. A group of children could compile these accounts prior to the assembly and the world's trouble-spots could be identified on a large map. Alternatively, you could use film footage of current hostilities from news broadcasts to introduce the assembly.

You could also consider following this assembly with one of the other assemblies in this book which relate to former winners of the Nobel Peace Prize. These include: Nelson Mandela (Assembly 12), Martin Luther King (Assembly 13) and Henry Dunant (Assembly 15). The Red Cross, who's story is in the next assembly, have won the Nobel Peace Prize on three occasions.

Five Star Assembly ✪✪✪✪✪

To enrich the assembly you could ask the children to research previous winners of the Nobel Peace Prize and make presentations about them in assembly. This could be through PowerPoint presentations or other media. For more recent winners, film footage maybe available that can be downloaded for the presentation.

Consider closing the assembly with Haim G. Ginnott's famous letter to teachers:

Dear Teachers:

I am a survivor of a concentration camp. My eyes saw what no person should witness. Gas chambers built by learned engineers. Children poisoned by educated physicians. Infants killed by trained nurses. Women and babies shot and burned by high school and college graduates.

So I am suspicious of education. My request is: help your students become more human. Your efforts must never produce learned monsters, skilled psychopaths, or educated Eichmanns. Reading, writing, and arithmetic are important only if they serve to make our children more humane.[1]

1   From Haim G. Ginott, *Teacher and Child: A Book for Parents and Teachers* (New York: Macmillan, 1975).

75

Themes: **The Red Cross**

Timing: **General or International Red Cross Day (8 May) or as near as possible to the International Day of the Disappeared (30 August)**

15.
I Can Either Do Nothing or I Can Do Something: The Birth of the Red Cross

During the assembly you could use a small Team of Experts with laptop or tablet computers to find additional information about the Red Cross, how it was formed and some of its achievements.

Three Star Assembly ✪✪✪

Script

The image shows that the earth is scorched and there is no immediate sign of rain. As a consequence, the crops will fail leaving the inhabitants of an African village without food. When a disaster strikes, one of the first organisations to get through and provide aid is the Red Cross. The symbol of the Red Cross or the Red Crescent is easily recognized. It is an organization that has done great deeds and been awarded the Nobel Peace Prize on three occasions. Today we are going to look at how it was formed. However, we first need to consider an important issue.

When you see something that is wrong in the world you can either ignore it or you can do something about it. Sometimes we might make a small gesture like a charitable donation. On other occasions we might try to do something bigger. However, it would be very sad if we did nothing.

Imagine you are watching television and the news broadcasts are showing film footage of a natural disaster such as an earthquake, flood or famine. One of the first organizations to arrive and offer support is the International Red Cross. Their workers, many of whom are volunteers, are seen quickly bringing relief to people in very difficult situations. Similarly, when soldiers or civilians are wounded on the battlefield you will often find members of the Red Cross there seeking to provide medical assistance.

Now let us come back to this country. Imagine that you see an ambulance hurtling at great speed down a road. On the side of the vehicle you may well see the sign of the red cross. You may also see the red cross on the uniform of a nurse. The Red Cross provides much of the first aid training in the UK and other countries. Those who access this training are taught how to provide life-saving treatment when somebody is seriously hurt.

But what is the Red Cross and why do they always seem to be in the right place at the right time?

Story

The story of the Red Cross goes back to the summer of 1859 and a war in Italy. A Swiss businessman called Henry Dunant was in the north of the country and he witnessed the terrible aftermath of the Battle of Solferino. There were so many wounded and injured soldiers desperately in need of medical attention (around 22,000) but there was hardly anybody to help. Soldiers were now dying not because of the battle but because there was nobody to look after them. There were too few doctors and nurses and insufficient medical supplies. Henry was alarmed that men could do this much damage to their fellow men. He also thought, well, I can either do nothing or I can do something.

Henry Dunant wrote a book called *A Memory of Solferino*, which told the story of what he had observed and why there was a need for a medical organization that would always be ready to provide support and medical attention during wars or other disasters. Henry Dunant was passionate in this belief and worked hard to bring his dream to reality. In 1864 he founded the International Red Cross.

The first meeting took place in Geneva, Switzerland, which was Henry Dunant's home town. There were representatives from countries from all over the world. Over the following weeks and months, agreements were made about how countries should treat prisoners of war and that medical staff must never be attacked during battles. However, for this to happen, there had to be a way of recognizing those offering urgent medical support, and so a red cross was selected as the emblem (this is the reverse of the Swiss flag). In some Muslim countries, the Red Cross is replaced with the title and emblem of the Red Crescent.

In 1901, Henry Dunant was awarded the Nobel Peace Prize for his work. Today, the Red Cross not only provides workers in the case of extreme emergencies but they also plan appropriate actions for when an emergency occurs so the organization can react quickly.

Questions to consider:

- Let us just think about that statement that we began with: 'When you see something that is wrong in the world you can either ignore it or you can do something about it'. Which people in our community might need our help or support at this moment in time and what might we do to help them?

- What places in the world are currently exploring conflict, famine and drought? What do you think the Red Cross might be doing there, and is there anything you can do to help?

If you have used the Team of Experts model you could ask them to provide additional information at this stage.

Four Star Assembly ⭐⭐⭐☆

With extra time, you could ask children to use the Red Cross website to research where in the world the organization is currently working to bring relief under very difficult circumstances. Children could also do specific research about the work of the Red Cross at home. The Red Cross proudly announce that they help huge numbers of people in the United Kingdom who are affected by flood, fire or health issues. The information could be used either in this assembly or at a subsequent one.

Five Star Assembly ⭐⭐⭐⭐☆

Script

There are two special days in the Red Cross calendar. One is 8 May, which is International Red Cross Day, when the work of the organization is celebrated all over the world. The second date is 30 August, which is the International Day of the Disappeared. This commemorates those people who have disappeared or been lost to their families as a result of war or natural disaster. It is also a day to remember some of the success stories of the Red Cross in reuniting people who have been parted from each other. There are many stories on their website, but here is one to help you on your way.

Sokonan Keita lived in the Ivory Coast when she suddenly found herself in great danger because of her political activism. She was forced to flee for her own safety but she left in a hurry and became separated from her children in the process. Before long she found herself on a flight to London where she sought safety as a refugee. For two years she was separated from her children and found it very difficult to find out anything about them. But then the Red Cross stepped in. One of their aims is to reunite families who have become separated. Eventually Sokonan was taken to an airport and told to wait at the arrival gate for a very special surprise. Can you imagine how she felt as her two children walked towards her?

16.
What Happens If Sea Levels Rise?

Three Star Assembly ⭐⭐⭐

> During the assembly you could use a small Team of Experts with laptop or tablet computers to find additional information about the causes of global warming and its potential impact.

Script

Take a look at the photograph of Manhattan, New York. The buildings are the striking feature, but also consider the Hudson River and the sea beyond it. Can you see how close the sea is to the base of the buildings? All is calm and peaceful in the picture, but in the autumn of 2012 the people who live and work in this area headed for higher ground as the deadly Hurricane Sandy approached. They were right to move as the hurricane brought surges in the sea level that flooded and devastated the cityscape you are looking at. The New York Subway flooded, as did the ground floor of many buildings. After the event, a Hurricane Task Force reported on the need to take climate change into account when planning for future storms, especially how rising sea levels will worsen the effects of storm-induced flooding.

The following story explores what might happen if we don't take the threat of global warming and rising sea levels seriously.

Story

The year is 2120. Jo has just emerged from her office on the twenty-third floor of the Empire State Building and is about to board her solar-powered boat to cruise through the streets of New York to the apartment block where she lives. Others are making their way home on their hover-boards, skimming through the air at a constant height of 30 centimetres above water level in the streets. It is a busy time of year in New York, with many tourists riding in the old gondolas which were shipped to the city from Venice after the water levels rose so high. The tourist department now markets the city as 'America's High-Rise Venice'. Jo finds herself thinking about the antique DVDs she has been watching with her great-grandfather. These include movies set in New York before the floods: a strange era when the streets were filled with bright yellow taxis, cars and motorcycles and people walked around on foot because the streets were dry. The films had been made in the early part of the twenty-first century – a time when scientists had given their warnings about global warming but too few people had listened.

What do you think could have happened to cause the streets of many of the world's great cities to flood?

In the hundred years between 1911 and 2011 the earth's temperature had increased by about 0.75°C. At the time this did not sound like very much, but it had a huge effect on the planet. It caused sea levels to rise by 15–20 centimetres. Some people thought that the Earth was simply getting warmer but there was nothing that could be done, so we should just carry on living as we had been. Others disagreed. Scientists had been warning that global warming could mean that huge areas of ice around the Arctic and Greenland would melt, causing the volume of water in the oceans to rise substantially. They believed that the use of fossil fuels, such as oil and gas, were causing the problem. Cars, airplanes, power stations and factories used huge quantities of fossil fuels every day and this was partly responsible for the warming of the earth and rising sea levels.

In the early part of the twenty-first century, scientists predicted that if sea levels continued to rise, some of our great coastal cities would be lost and some of our finest and most fertile low-lying farmland would become flooded. This would mean more people living in less space and with less land to grow food. Huge numbers of people faced losing their homes and there were fears that there might not be enough food, so starvation could increase.

Today, there are large-scale actions that governments can take to reduce global warming. For example, governments can commit to a reduction in the use of fossil fuels such as coal, gas and oil; they can ensure that energy efficiency improves in vehicles and buildings; and they can make sure that money is invested in renewable energy sources such as wind and solar power. Many countries have signed pledges to do this – one of the best-known ones is the Kyoto Protocol. However, there are many small things that you and I might do to reduce global warming. Here come the top examples:

+ Reduce, reuse and recycle wherever possible.

+ Reduce the use of heating and air conditioning systems.

+ Change to environmentally friendly light bulbs.

+ Drive less and bike or walk more.

+ Buy energy efficient products (especially when they have cut down on packaging).

+ Use less hot water.

+ Use the off switch whenever possible.

+ Plant a tree because plants absorb carbon dioxide and give off oxygen.

Once the commitment has been made in your school, children could then make contact with other schools in the locality using persuasive letters to see if they will make similar pledges. Alternatively, use the Internet to sign up schools in other parts of the country or world.

If you used the Team of Experts model you could ask them to provide additional information at this point to emphasise the importance of their commitment.

Four Star Assembly ★★★★

Questions to consider:

■ Take another look at the image – what small, specific things can children and schools do to reduce global warming and make the world's low-lying areas safer?

■ If our school were to draw up an environmental commitment, what would we write in it?

■ Can we think of a title for this commitment using six powerful words?

There are images available on the Internet of what would happen to some of the world's largest cities if sea levels rise. The following cities are particularly at risk: Mumbai and Calcutta in India; Guangzhou and Shanghai in China; Miami, New Orleans and New York City in the United States; Ho Chi Minh City in Vietnam; Osaka and Kobe in Japan; and Alexandria in Egypt. Low-lying coastal regions in developing nations such as Bangladesh, Vietnam, India and China are also vulnerable, as are some island nations. You could ask the children to research the populations of these cities or countries and work out the total number of people who are at risk of losing their homes and may need to immigrate.

Five Star Assembly ⭐⭐⭐⭐⭐

Script

Did you know that rich developed countries, such as Britain and the United States, make up just 15% of the world's population, but historically they are responsible for 75% of the global carbon dioxide emissions, which could lead to sea levels rising? The poorest 10% of the world's people contribute less than 1%.

Therefore, the rich countries of the world could be responsible for certain inhabited islands disappearing under the sea. If time allows, the children could research which islands will be affected by rising sea levels (e.g. the Philippines, Indonesia, Tuvalu, Vanuatu).

> You could project an image of an island onto an interactive whiteboard and then start to colour over them in blue to demonstrate what will happen if sea levels continue to rise.

> The children may be particularly interested in the work of Greenpeace, which has campaigned hard to bring about environmental change.

Greenpeace seek to defend the natural world and promote peace by investigating, exposing and confronting environmental abuse and championing environmentally responsible solutions. Greenpeace don't believe that climate change is inevitable – they consider that we have the knowledge, skills and technologies to get out of this difficult situation. However, they believe that all over the world people must wake up to the dangers and reduce their use of fossil fuels and replace it with power from clean energy.

Greenpeace have had three famous ships called *Rainbow Warrior* I, II and III. The final one is still in use. They have been used to bring the world's attention to particular environmental problems. They would sail the ship to a location where they believed destruction or damage was taking place. They would then protest about what was happening, but always in a peaceful and non-violent way. However, they would always seek to educate and inform the world about what was happening.

> The children could research some of the campaigns that Greenpeace have been involved in and also some of the stories of the *Rainbow Warrior* ships.

> Greenpeace claim the organization is based on traditional Quaker principles, which could lead to another area of research for the children.

17.
The USA and the Kyoto Protocol

Three Star Assembly ✪✪✪

During the assembly you could use a small Team of Experts with laptop or tablet computers to find additional information about the types of pollution caused by road traffic.

Script

Take a look at the photograph of one of the vehicles on our road today. We will talk about it later, but for now imagine the scene of a motorway filled with fast moving traffic. The good news is the traffic is moving because we have all sat, motionless, in our cars when we have been in a huge traffic jam. On these occasions, we are polluting the air and burning the earth's resources but going nowhere. Environmental Protection UK tells us that there are 34 million vehicles on our roads today, of which 28 million are cars. Road transport accounts for 22% of carbon dioxide transmissions and is also a major contributor to climate change. Motor vehicles bring other problems too. For example, they seriously affect air quality because of the emissions of nitrogen oxides, carbon monoxide and hydrocarbons, which affect the health of people, animals and vegetation. Short journeys which can often be avoided tend to cause the most environmental damage.

Story

The motorway is busy today. Traffic is roaring along and a constant rumbling is in the air. Cars are racing past in the fast lanes while huge lorries trundle along more slowly. Many of them have messages emblazoned on the side stating that they are reducing carbon emissions. One lorry displays the message, 'We've reduced our fuel emissions. That's a lorry load off your mind', followed by the message, 'Plan A because there is no Plan B'. Next comes another heavy goods vehicle proudly proclaiming it is using biogas to reduce carbon emissions. Yet another claims it is aerodynamically designed in order to reduce carbon emissions. At the motorway junction, a hybrid bus joins the nearside lane. The signs alongside its side proudly proclaim that it partly runs on electricity to reduce pollution.

These things are happening because people all over the world are concerned about greenhouse gases. These are gases that trap heat in the atmosphere. Some of them occur naturally but others are a result of human activity, such as the burning of fossil fuels like wood, coal, oil and natural gas. The increase in greenhouse gases adds to global warming because heat from the sun is radiated back into the earth's atmosphere. In the long term, this could cause sea levels to rise, leading to the loss of cities, agricultural land and natural habitats.

Because so many countries in the world were concerned about the increase in greenhouse gases and global warming, they signed an agreement to reduce the emission of greenhouse gases in 1997. This agreement was called the Kyoto Protocol. This treaty, negotiated by more than 100 countries over a decade, called for the thirty-eight largest industrial nations to reduce their emissions of greenhouse gases by 2012 to 5.2% below the levels in 1990. All those taking part thought this could be achieved and that it would make a real difference. It is because of the Kyoto Protocol that you now see signs and announcements from some of the world's biggest companies indicating that they are working to reduce carbon emissions.

The United States is one of the world's largest producers of greenhouse gases: in 2002, with just 4% of the world's population, it created nearly 25% of the world's greenhouse gases.[1] The United States has a large landmass and this means that people have to travel long distances by road and air in order to transport goods or to meet each other. However, many of the cars on US roads are large and therefore use larger quantities of fuel. The country's power stations and factories add further to the production of greenhouse gases.

However, the United States has refused to ratify the Kyoto Protocol, and in 2001, President George Bush provoked much criticism by rejecting the principles for tackling climate change on which it is based. Successive American governments have said that if they agreed to the reductions recommended it would badly affect the US economy and this might mean people losing their jobs. President Bush said that the American people should make

---

1 See http://news.bbc.co.uk/1/hi/world/americas/1820523.stm (accessed 28 August 2012).

the rules for the people of America and not people from other countries. He added that conforming to the agreement was not in US interests. Since that time other countries, including Canada, Japan and Russia, have refused to adopt further Kyoto targets.

Questions to consider:

- Take a look at the image – what words would you use to describe the scene and what are some of the dangers of busy, congested roads?

- Do you think the United States should have made a commitment to the other countries of the world to reduce greenhouse gases?

- Should all countries make a commitment to reduce greenhouse gases?

- Is it sometimes right that other countries influence laws elsewhere in the world in order to achieve a greater good?

- Take another look at the image; the lorry proudly proclaims it is reducing fuel emissions. What do you think it means by 'Plan A because there is no Plan B'?

If you used the Team of Experts model you could ask them to provide additional information at this point.

Four Star Assembly ✪✪✪✪

The children could write to local or national companies to ask what they are currently doing to reduce emissions. If the children really want to push their luck, they could ask if the business is prepared to fund a wind turbine or solar panels for the school, because this would represent a tremendous commitment on their behalf as well as excellent advertising!

Five Star Assembly ✪✪✪✪✪

The learning could be extended further by asking the children to design and test their own aerodynamic and environmentally friendly vehicles, which could be demonstrated in the assembly or at a subsequent one.

If the notion of a wind turbine or solar panels really interests the children, then they could consider setting up their own campaign to acquire them on behalf of the school. This could include lobbying relevant individuals/organizations, writing persuasive letters or running their own enterprise projects to contribute towards the costs.

18.

What can the World Learn from the Poppy Fields of Flanders?

During the assembly you could use a small Team of Experts with laptop or tablet computers to find our which nations have tombs dedicated to unknown soldiers and information about the International Day of Peace.

Three Star Assembly ✪✪✪

Script

Nations all over the world have ways of remembering members of their armed forces who have lost their lives in wars and battles over many years. Many countries place wreaths at the tomb of an unknown soldier. There are thirty-eight tombs to unknown warriors in each of the five continents and covering all the major faiths. The principle is that an ordinary soldier who has lost his life in battle should receive the same funeral as a king. One of the most famous is at the Arc de Triomphe in Paris. In Chile and the Ukraine there are also tombs to unknown sailors.

Many of these tombs were set up after the First World War, which was responsible for the deaths of over 10 million soldiers, including 1.7 million Russians, 1.3 million French, 1.7 million Germans, 1.3 million Austrians and 900,000 from Britain. Much of this war was fought in fields in Northern Europe. When the war was over, often the first plants to grow back in these fields were poppies. It is a special species of flower because it only grows when the earth is disturbed.

In November 1918, a poem by Canadian military doctor John McCrae, called 'In Flanders Fields', inspired American humanitarian Moina Michael to wear and distribute poppies in honour of fallen soldiers. Around the same time, poppies were sold to support those orphans and war widows. Today, poppies are sold in over 120 countries to support those who have been injured or affected by war. The Royal British Legion adopted the poppy in 1921. The following story demonstrates the futility of war and especially relates to British soldiers during the Great War.

Story

The year was 1914 and Britain was heading towards war. As the army was relatively small at this time, the government set about recruiting 500,000 volunteers. Many cities set about trying to build their own battalion of local men. Liverpool moved first and quickly recruited enough men to create four battalions. Accrington, Derby and Sheffield quickly followed. Then came other companies like the Glasgow Tramways Battalion and East Grinstead Sportsman's Battalion, which became known as 'pals battalions'. All were keen to show loyalty to their country in a war that they believed would be over in a matter of months and from which they would return home as heroes.

Willie McBride was one such man. He joined the huge queues of men prepared to fight for their country. He spent most of 1914 and 1915 training in Britain before being shipped to the trenches of France in 1916. Willie had spent two years being trained but, like thousands of other soldiers, he was dead in just ten minutes. On 1 July 1916 he, along with hundreds of other volunteers, was ordered to march forward in formation across 'no man's land' towards the German enemy lines in order to capture their territory. They walked straight into a hail of bullets. There were 60,000 casualties and 20,000 deaths. The Leeds Pals lost 750 out of the 900 men in their ranks. Out of the 720 Accrington Pals, 584 were killed, wounded or went missing. The Grimsby Chums and Sheffield City Battalion lost half of their men.

Willie McBride was buried in one of the 243 military cemeteries on the Somme battlefield. Many of the pals who left home with great optimism, and who were expecting to return home as heroes, are at rest in these graveyards.

Many years later, on a warm summer's day, a traveller walked into one such cemetery and found himself looking at Willie McBride's gravestone and asking himself questions about his life and whether we really did learn any lessons for the future. These questions and answers were later turned into a song called 'The Green Fields of France'.

Each year we remember those who have died in conflict when we buy poppies, but have you ever paused to wonder why we use the poppy out of all the flowers? During the First World War trenches were dug into the fields. The soldiers lived in the trenches below the ground until they were ordered to advance on enemy lines. Poppy seeds are unusual as they lie dormant and don't grow unless the earth is disturbed. The trenches and bombardments had that effect on the poppy seeds. When the war was over, the battlefields of Northern Europe were covered in thousands of red poppies.

There is a famous song about these fields called 'The Green Fields of France' by Eric Bogle. It has been described by former British Prime Minister Tony Blair as the greatest anti-war song written. Here are the opening lines:

<Show lyrics. For example www. http://celtic-lyrics.com/lyrics/225.html YouTube also have a video>

<Well, how do you do …
Willie McBride was it slow and obscene?>

The song poses many questions about war that are still important today. It was written in 1976 about the soldiers from both sides that lost their lives in the trenches of the First World War. The song focuses on a soldier called Willie McBride. The records do not say who this soldier was, where he came from or how he died, but the story above could be his story.

Now let's go back to the words of the song:

<Remainder of lyrics starting Now, Willie McBride …
and again, and again, and again>

The song tells of the futility, pain and misery of war and how, nearly a century on, soldiers and civilians continue to lose their lives every year.

You can extend the assembly further by playing the whole song. The most famous versions are by The Furey Brothers and Davey Arthur but other recordings are also available on the Internet.

Questions to consider:

■ Do you think the Great War was really justifiable?

■ What would you want to say to the politicians who caused it?

■ What should we learn from the story?

If you used the Team of Experts model you could ask them to feedback information at this point.

Four Star Assembly ★★★★

There is a very strong argument that any assembly of this nature should also be treated as an opportunity to promote world peace. Each year, on 21 September, the United Nations holds an International Day of Peace. The day is devoted to commemorating and strengthening the ideals of peace both within and among all nations and peoples. In 2013, the UN General Secretary, Ban Ki-moon said of the day: 'It is not enough to teach children how to read, write and count. Education has to cultivate mutual respect for others and the world in which we live, and help people forge more just, inclusive and peaceful societies.'

Five Star Assembly ★★★★★

It would also be possible to look at the story of the white poppy. The first white poppies were introduced in 1933 by the Cooperative Women's Guild. They selected white because they felt that it symbolized peace. In the centre of the first white poppies it said 'No more war' rather than the words 'Haig Fund'. However, many people thought that the white poppy was an insult to those who had lost their lives so bravely. The organizers said that this was never their intention. The purpose of the white poppy was to remember the dead and injured, but also to hope that there would be no more wars.

The white poppy remains controversial to this day. The children could research their history further and consider whether or not they think they are a good idea.

19.

Big Issue, Sir? A Hand Up and Not a Handout

Three Star Assembly ⭐⭐⭐

During the assembly you could use a small Team of Experts with laptop or tablet computers to find additional information about the homeless, The Big Issue or charities like Shelter.

Script

Take a look at the image. Can you start to describe the woman in the scene. She is either homeless or vulnerably housed. She wears a high visibility jacket because she is in danger of attack. She is smiling now but before the picture was taken a group of teenagers went by shouting 'scrounger scrounger!' She is selling *The Big Issue* but she wants to rescue her life. The theme today is homeless people or those who are extremely vulnerable. Is it possible to find out more about how many homeless people live in your area, how old these people are and why they had to live on the streets. There are many charities which work to provide support to the people affected by homelessness. Today we are going to explore the difference between offering somebody a hand up and a handout.

You could start with these questions:

■ What do you think is meant by offering somebody a 'hand up'?

■ Can you think of occasions when you have offered somebody a 'hand up'?

■ What do you understand by the term handout?

Here are two stories about homeless people. They take place a hundred years apart.

Story

Sadly, in cities around the world, each night homeless people are left to sleep outdoors. You will all have heard of Thomas Barnardo. In the 1860s, he was about to leave England to do missionary work with sick people in China, but he became increasingly concerned about the numbers of children in Britain who had no home to go to. Many were orphans and had no money for either food or clothes. He was determined to improve the life chances of these children and so he set about raising funds from some of the richest people in order to bring about change. He wanted these children to be fed and clothed but, above all else, educated so that they could go on to live useful lives.

The first of Dr Barnardo's homes was opened in London in 1870. By the time he died in 1905 he had 112 similar homes. He opened a special hospital home with medical facilities for the seriously ill and convalescent homes for children recovering from illness. These were often by the sea. Once a child raised in a Dr Barnardo's home reached 13 or 14 years of age, they started to be taught a trade so that they could later gain employment. They were given a hand up and not a handout.

Now let's move forward to the present day and consider the plight of an elderly homeless woman trying to sell *Big Issue* magazines on the streets of a city in the UK, Japan or Australia. She is trying hard to change her life for the better but is abused by passers-by who call her a 'scrounger'.

Twenty years ago, a wealthy businessman called Gordon Roddick found himself thinking about the hundreds of homeless people in Britain. He had no reason to worry about these people – he was rich and lived in a beautiful big house. Maybe he was standing outside one of his shops while he was thinking. He had worked hard in life and built up a chain of shops called The Body Shop.

Gordon Roddick knew he wanted to do something positive that would make a real difference, just like Thomas Barnado had done all those years before. He wanted to help homeless people, but he also knew that the real challenge was to find a way to help them help themselves. The 'big issue' was how to give them a hand up and not a handout.

And those two words, *big issue*, provided his solution. You have probably seen people selling magazines by that name on our busy shopping streets. I wonder if any of you have ever stopped to buy one or whether you know anything about the people selling them. (At this you could pause and get some responses from the children.)

The people selling *Big Issue* magazines are receiving a hand up and not a handout. They are homeless or vulnerably housed people who buy the magazines for £1 and sell them for £2, in the hope that they can start to turn their lives around. By doing this, they are starting to earn a legitimate wage that will help them to move away from homelessness. They begin to take control of their lives by starting to run their own small business. They are trained to manage sales so they build up their finances and, above everything else, this process boosts their self-confidence for the future.

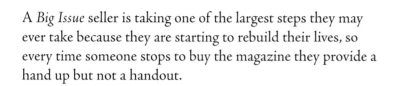

A *Big Issue* seller is taking one of the largest steps they may ever take because they are starting to rebuild their lives, so every time someone stops to buy the magazine they provide a hand up but not a handout.

Questions to consider:

■ Take a look at the image one more time. Can you describe the woman and her situation in six really powerful words that come together to make a very short story?

■ Which do you think is a better way of supporting homeless people – a hand up or a handout?

■ Can you think of other ways that local authorities might support homeless and vulnerable people?

■ Are there more things that you or I could do to support homeless or vulnerable people?

If you used the Team of Experts model you could now ask them to provide any relevant information about homeless people or the work of the Big Issue.

Four Star Assembly ⭐⭐⭐⭐

The Big Issue website is updated on a regular basis but it includes a promotional film about how The Big Issue works which could be shared with the children. It also includes up-to-date stories about people who have taken the first steps in transforming their lives. These could also be used to bring a real-life element to the assembly.

Five Star Assembly ⭐⭐⭐⭐⭐

Take the assembly to the next level by concluding it with 'Streets of London' by Ralph McTell. The song is worth listening to in its own right. It features a number of characters who are lonely and possibly homeless. You could focus on one of the characters in the song, perhaps the one whose memories are fading with the medal ribbons that he wears. Ask the children to consider how he may have earned the medals.

20.
Buy One Get One Free:
Is It a Good Thing or a Bad Thing?

Three Star Assembly ★ ★ ★

During the assembly you could use a small Team of Experts with laptop or tablet computers to find additional information about how much food is wasted and ends up in landfill sites.

Script

This image shows a tasty looking treat – one which many of us might take for granted. In many parts of the world there is a plentiful supply of food and people can eat as much as they want and any waste is simply thrown away. Perhaps we should be more careful. Food supplies in rich Western nations are dependent on a complex system of transportation – if fuel supplies were halted our supermarket shelves would start to look bare in three days. In 1997, Mexico was hit by the tortilla riots when 70,000 people took to the streets because the price of flat corn bread, which was eaten by poorer people, rose by 400%. Many people blamed the richer United States, which was able to pay higher prices for the corn, partly to make bio-fuels. Today's story looks at one way in which we can be more responsible about food supply and waste.

Story

Mrs Johnson was an elderly woman and she was at her local supermarket. Standing in front of the fruit counter she looked very confused. To the left were 500 gram packs of strawberries marked '£2 each or two for £3'. To the right were 500 gram packs of raspberries marked '£2 each but buy one and get one free'. In the middle were 500 gram packs of blackberries also at £2 each but marked 'three for the price of two'. Mrs Johnson liked strawberries, raspberries and blackberries, but she just stood there staring and trying to work out which deal offered the best value for money.

If you were to help Mrs Johnson, which one would you say offered the best value for money?

The supermarket manager was watching Mrs Johnson and, seeing the puzzled look on her face, thought he would offer his advice. He believed this was a kind thing to do. 'I think the blackberries are the best deal,' he said in a gentle voice.

'Well, I think it is appalling,' said Mrs Johnson angrily, 'and I'm going to write to your store manager about this.' Then she walked off.

I wonder if you have any ideas as to why she left the store in such an angry mood.

Mrs Johnson may have been elderly but she certainly was not confused. The simple truth is that she only wanted one packet of fruit because the rest would have been wasted. She would have thrown it away and this worried her. Mrs Johnson knew that while people in some parts of the developing world are starving, a typical family in Britain throws away £680 worth of food every year. Much of it goes into landfill and helps to create a mountain of wasted food that is worth £12 billion and weighs over seven million tonnes.[1] The most common food waste is potatoes, bread, apples and salad products.

Mrs Johnson had a long memory. During the Second World War food had been rationed and she was fairly sure that her grandmother, who had been a member of the Women's Institute, had campaigned to restrict food waste back in the 1920s.

When Mrs Johnson arrived home she read an article in her newspaper. It said that supermarkets were contributing to the problem of food waste through 'multi-pack offers' of perishable food because frequently people couldn't eat the food quickly enough before it started to go off. The exposé also reported that if the buy-one-get-one-free offers didn't exist, there would be fewer lorries on the roads delivering food that wasn't really wanted and consequently less packaging would be thrown away.

Mrs Johnson was now very angry and felt she ought do something about the situation. But what should she do? Do you have any suggestions?

---

1 See http://www.bbc.co.uk/news/uk-15733624 (accessed 5 August 2013).

Questions to consider:

- Much of the food in supermarkets is labelled with 'best before' dates. Sometimes this just leads to food being thrown away. Do you think there are more responsible actions that could be taken?

- Supermarkets often have buy-one-get-one-free special offers, but what else could they do that would be less wasteful?

- Do you believe multi-pack special offers are a good idea or not?

If you used the Team of Experts model you could ask them to provide additional information at this point.

Four Star Assembly ⭐⭐⭐⭐

Five Star Assembly ⭐⭐⭐⭐⭐

The assembly could be extended in a variety of ways. For example, prior to the assembly you could work with one of the classes in school and ask them to weigh the amount of food waste each family disposes of during a week. From there it might be feasible to calculate the amount that the whole school throws away each week and then each year. It may be possible to see if Mrs Johnson's thoughts about food waste were accurate. Perhaps the food could be separated into the waste that comes from multi-pack purchases and the rest.

Another extension activity might be to ask the children to write letters imagining what Mrs Johnson might say to the owners of the supermarket. The outcomes of these activities could then be fed into the assembly.

The issue of food waste has been a significant one for the last century. You could demonstrate this point by collecting samples of posters from the First and Second World Wars (these are readily available on the Internet).

Another option would be to compare the amount of food a typical family consumes today compared with the rations a similar family may have received during the Second World War. The children could even try cooking some wartime recipes.

Finally you could also explore the advantages of composting fruit/vegetable waste as opposed to sending it to landfill.

21.

Our Wheelie Bin is Full of Energy Today; or Let's be Smelly and Watch 500 Hours of Television

Three Star Assembly ✦ ✦ ✦

During the assembly you could use a small Team of Experts with laptop or tablet computers to find additional information about the importance of recycling and the problems associated with landfill sites.

Script

In this image, a huge machine is crushing cars which were once somebody's pride and joy but now are no longer required and therefore have been thrown away as rubbish. The good news is that much of this waste can be recycled. However, what really happens to the stuff we throw away and can we use our waste better?

Story

This is a true story about what happens to the things we throw away, but first here comes a question and the answer. Have you ever dropped a bottle of tomato ketchup on the floor? If it was a glass bottle, and it broke, it might have left a nasty mess on the floor. If you were lucky, and it was a plastic bottle, it would remain in one piece and there wouldn't be a stain in sight. These bottles are made from polyethylene terephthalate (PET). However, when plastic bottles are thrown away they may well leave a stain on the environment. This is because the bottle is virtually indestructible. The ketchup bottle, along with millions of others, will be around forever more.

Information from the Environment Agency tells us that, on average, each person in the UK throws away their own body weight in rubbish every seven weeks. If you could pile up the glass bottles we throw away each year and put them one on top of the other, you could make six pillars that reached to the moon. If you took all the aluminium cans we throw away each year and made them into a very long line, it would stretch around the earth nine times. That is masses and masses of rubbish, but where does it all go? This problem is replicated in countries all over the world. Could the surface of the earth just become covered with the rubbish we throw away?

In the past our rubbish simply went to landfill sites and was dumped in the ground in places like old quarries and then forgotten about. People probably thought it would just rot away. But the reality is that much of it doesn't. Some waste will decompose, but other materials just degrade by breaking down into smaller and smaller pieces.

- If you throw away a paper bag it will take about one week to decompose.

- If you throw away a woollen sock it will take about a year to decompose.

- If you throw away an aluminium can it will take fifty years to decompose.

- If you throw away a disposable nappy it will take 550 years to degrade.

- If you throw away a plastic bag it will take 1,000 years to degrade.

- If you throw away a plastic bucket it will take 99,999 years to degrade.

- If you throw away a glass bottle it will take 149,000 years to degrade.

- If you throw away a styrofoam cup it will take 750,000,000 years to degrade.

But did you know that your wheelie bin is actually full of energy? The UK Energy Saving website tells us that, on average, each family in the UK throws away six trees worth of paper each year, but paper is very easily recycled and it takes 70% less energy to make recycled paper than new paper.

Glass bottles can be recycled several times without ever losing their purity. It also takes far less energy to make a bottle from recycled glass. The energy saved by recycling one glass bottle would power a light bulb for an hour.

Aluminium cans can be easily recycled. The energy needed to make one new aluminium can is enough to recycle twenty old cans. This energy would be sufficient to allow you to watch a television or computer screen for three hours.

So, if you take recycling seriously, not only might you save some of the world's mineral resources but you could also save electrical energy. If you take the wheelie bin of an average family and recycle as much as possible over the year, with the energy saved you could:

+ Heat the water for 500 baths.

+ Heat the water for 3,500 showers.

+ Or, if you prefer to remain dirty or smelly (and can keep awake!), you could watch television for 5,000 hours.

So, if we recycle things very carefully we can do the earth a great deal of good. Every time we recycle we are not only saving the earth's resources but also preventing 58 million tonnes of harmful gases going into the atmosphere through the energy that has been saved. It would take 64,046 square miles of rainforest to absorb these gases. In short, by recycling we are helping to prevent global warming.

Questions to consider:

■ Look again at the giant machine compacting the old cars – can you think of other things that may be difficult to dispose of?

■ How could manufacturers be more responsible about the packaging they use?

■ Can you sum up the key messages in this assembly in six powerful words?

If you used the Team of Experts model you could ask them to provide additional information at this point.

Four Star Assembly ⭐⭐⭐⭐

You could add some interest to the assembly by building up a collection of the items listed in the story and asking the children to predict which ones would take the longest time to decompose or degrade.

Five Star Assembly ⭐⭐⭐⭐⭐

You could also have fun with the mathematics: if I wanted to watch three hours of television each night for a week, and I had to pay in recycled aluminium cans, how many would I need? You could extend it further by making alternative versions of the three times table: one recycled can = 3 hours of TV, two recycled cans = 6 hours of TV and so on.

22.
666 Reservoirs and Rising

Three Star Assembly ● ● ●

Script

Take a look at the image – a reservoir filled with water and pipes ready to transport it to our homes for a whole variety of purposes. In many parts of the world fresh water is something that is taken for granted. However, as the global population rises and the climate changes, we may need to seek out new sources of water.

In early 2012, many parts of Britain were heading into drought. Reservoirs were starting to dry up, especially in the south of the country. On 21 February, *The Times* had the headline: 'Millions of Families Hit by the Worst Drought in 30 years' and 'South-East Faces Hosepipe Ban as Rivers Dry Up'.

What is very unusual is that after the winter we would expect water to be in plentiful supply in the UK. Britain has had previous occasions when water has been in short supply, but not usually in the winter months. However, our climate is changing and some experts predict that the amount of rainfall in the south-east of the country could reduce by one fifth over the next fifty years, while the overall population in the country could increase by ten million. Therefore, we need to start to think about water in a different way – and we may need more reservoirs like the one in the picture.

You could introduce the story below while sipping from a glass of water.

Story

Let us start our story in 1939 in the villages of Derwent and Ashopton in Derbyshire. If you were to look for them on a map today you wouldn't be able to find them because they have disappeared. They were beautiful villages: a meandering river flowed through their centres, there were attractive sandstone houses, a church stood in the centre of both villages and they were surrounded by farmland where animals grazed and farmers tended their crops.

The village of Ashopton disappeared in 1939. On 25 September of that year a final church service was held in Ashopton and the congregation sang a beautiful hymn called the 'The Day is Dying in the West', which is about the sun setting over God's beautiful creation. At the end of the hymn the people left the chapel, the door was locked and the people never returned. The village was demolished. Derwent suffered a similar fate in 1943.

The reason they were abandoned was that the villages were flooded – deliberately. Two huge dams were built to form reservoirs to supply fresh water to some of England's rapidly growing cities in Yorkshire and Lancashire. The sandstone buildings would never be seen again. However, during dry summers when water levels fall in the reservoir, the mighty church spire in Derwent, which was left intact, can be seen above the water line.

The same story was repeated in other parts of Britain during the 1920s, 1930s and 1940s. Our cities were getting bigger and the demand for water was rapidly increasing. New reservoirs were built as well as networks of pipes deep underground to bring precious water supplies to homes everywhere.

Currently there are 666 reservoirs that provide water to the 63 million people who live in Britain, and on average each of us uses 50 litres of water per day. We take for granted that clean water will come from the taps each time we turn them on. But there could be problems ahead and twenty-first century Britain has once again embarked on a scheme of building more reservoirs, enlarging existing ones and extending the network of pipes that move the water around. Maybe more people will have to relocate so that additional dams can be built and more land flooded for reservoirs.

Why do you think this might be? It isn't just because our cities are growing and new houses are being built. Nor is it because the population is rising. It is predominantly because our climate is changing. This means that water supplies will become less predictable. While some parts of the country will become drier, such as the south-east, flooding might also become a more regular occurrence in northern and western areas.

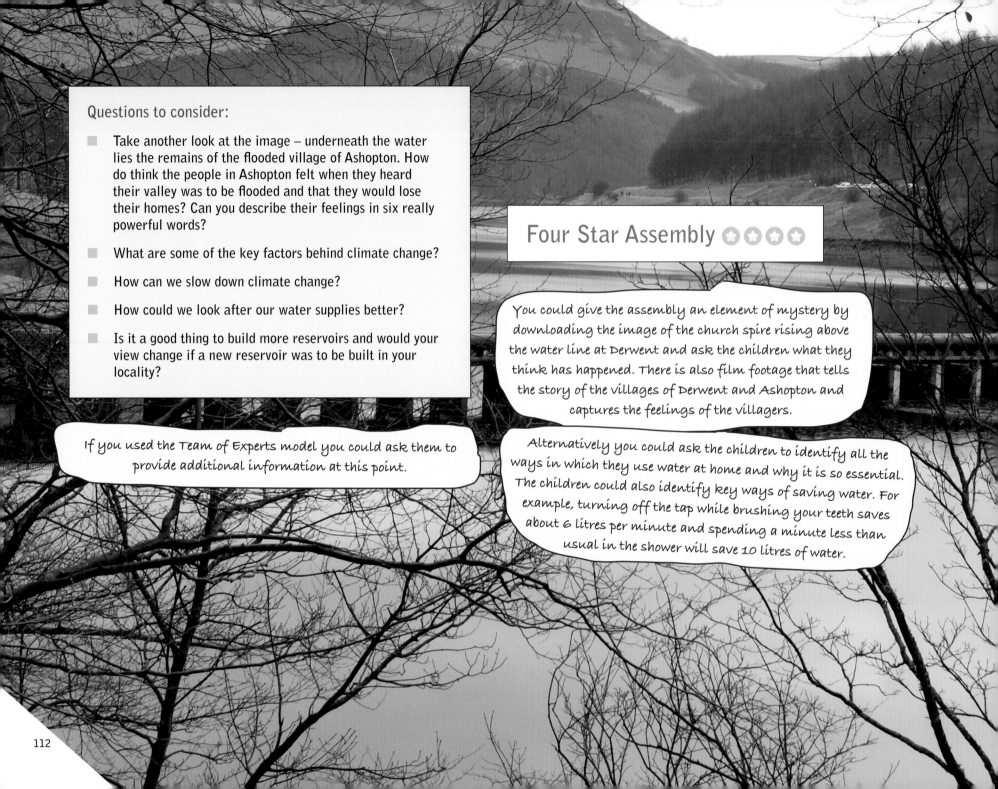

Questions to consider:

- Take another look at the image – underneath the water lies the remains of the flooded village of Ashopton. How do think the people in Ashopton felt when they heard their valley was to be flooded and that they would lose their homes? Can you describe their feelings in six really powerful words?

- What are some of the key factors behind climate change?

- How can we slow down climate change?

- How could we look after our water supplies better?

- Is it a good thing to build more reservoirs and would your view change if a new reservoir was to be built in your locality?

Four Star Assembly ⭐⭐⭐⭐

You could give the assembly an element of mystery by downloading the image of the church spire rising above the water line at Derwent and ask the children what they think has happened. There is also film footage that tells the story of the villages of Derwent and Ashopton and captures the feelings of the villagers.

If you used the Team of Experts model you could ask them to provide additional information at this point.

Alternatively you could ask the children to identify all the ways in which they use water at home and why it is so essential. The children could also identify key ways of saving water. For example, turning off the tap while brushing your teeth saves about 6 litres per minute and spending a minute less than usual in the shower will save 10 litres of water.

Five Star Assembly ✪ ✪ ✪ ✪ ✪

You could seek to develop increased empathy for the people who gave up their homes when the reservoirs were built. Try building an idyllic model village: use strips of blue paper to represent the meandering river, brown or grey for the roads and green to represent farmland – perhaps adding model farm animals to the scene. Make a crossroads at the centre of the village and use modelling clay to construct the buildings. While making the model, describe to the children how beautiful the village is and perhaps add stories about who might live there. You could enhance the effect by playing the music to 'The Day is Dying in the West' or close the assembly with this piece of music. Then dwell on the importance of people doing the right thing in order to help their country.

It is also possible to look at water supply in a global context (other assembly ideas exist in this book). The children could research a range of issues – for example, water scarcity is now critical in parts of Africa and Southeast Asia, but global warming is likely to increase problems in the Americas, Australia and New Zealand. Meanwhile, flooding is likely to increase in coastal regions.

23.
Not In My Back Yard:
The Story of a Wind Farm Nimby

Three Star Assembly ⭐⭐⭐

During the assembly you could use a small Team of Experts with laptop or tablet computers to find out additional information about occasions where there have been disagreements about the siting of wind turbines.

Script

Take a look at the wind turbines. Do you consider them to be a graceful and beautiful? Or do you view them as a scar on the landscape? You may think they are a wonderful source of sustainable energy or you may prefer your electricity to come from more established power stations.

A protester shouts 'Not in my back yard' at the top of his voice, but what is he complaining about? Let's find out more.

Most of the electricity we get from our power stations comes from burning fossil fuels such as gas or coal. Eventually, though, these resources will run out. There is also evidence that the carbon dioxide produced when burning them damages the environment. We therefore need to find our energy from other sources. Some of you may have had solar panels installed on your roof at home and others of you will have seen wind farms with giant turbines.

Britain is one of the windiest countries in Western Europe and this means it has the capacity to generate huge amounts of electricity cheaply from wind and without causing pollution or damage to the environment.

So, now put your hands up if you think that building wind farms is a good idea. Now keep your hands up if you still think it would be a good idea if the turbines were to be built near to your home.

Often people protest against the building of wind farms; while they think turbines are a good idea in principle, they don't want them erected near their homes. This is partly because it might spoil the view, cause shadow flicker or lead to turbine noise. Sometimes these people are sometimes called nimby's, which stands for 'not in my back yard'.

Story

The following story is true. Imagine a countryside scene: a series of small villages nestle by a stream and then the hills gently rise. From their homes the villagers get a tremendous view of the landscape. There are farmer's fields where animals graze. Public footpaths criss-cross the land which walkers use on a regular basis to enjoy the countryside and view the landscape. Animals such as badgers have made their home here. The meadows are full of a rich variety of wild flowers. Now plans have been announced to build four wind turbines two miles from the village. Many of the local people are objecting to the building of the wind farm because:

+ The 100-metre high turbines will spoil the view.
+ House prices will be reduced because people won't want to move into the area any more.
+ Some of the footpaths may have to be abandoned because the turbines would block the route.
+ The meadows may be badly damaged because heavy vehicles will need to drive around the hillside with machinery and parts for the turbines.
+ The habitats of wild animals could be lost.

+ There may be noise from the turbines that could stop people sleeping at night or even frighten farm animals.
+ Wind farms should not be placed in beautiful countryside.

However, other people like the idea of the wind turbines. They say:

+ It is an ideal location for the turbines because there is always a steady wind in the valley.
+ We need to stop burning coal and gas and use more renewable energy sources.
+ People will quickly get used to the wind turbines and they may create jobs because some people will get construction work at the site.
+ The turbines are not allowed to be noisy because there are regulations that prevent them from making too much noise.
+ We all need to contribute to the need to provide renewable energy.
+ Many other people have lived near power stations in the past and now it should be someone else's turn.

Questions to consider:

- So which side of the argument do you agree with, and why?

- If you are in favour of wind turbines can you express your argument in six powerful words?

- If you are against wind turbines can you express your argument in six powerful words?

- Would you add any restrictions about how near wind farms should be built to existing buildings?

- If a wind farm was to be built, how could we minimize the concerns of local people?

Alternatively, you could simply ask the children for their views. If your hall is big enough, you could ask them to move to different parts of the hall depending on their opinions: one corner for those who agree there should be a wind farm; another corner for those who partly agree; the third corner for those who partly disagree; and the final corner for those who totally disagree. You could ask the children to explain why they have selected a particular corner to see if they can persuade any other pupils to change their mind.

If you used the Team of Experts model you could ask them to provide the additional information at this point.

Four Star Assembly ✪✪✪✪

There is a really powerful short film called Dangle, produced by the British Film Industry, which you could use to introduce the assembly. (Take care to find the right film as there are others with the same title!). The film explores actions and consequences and the misguided behaviour of one man who turns out the light on the world. You could show the film and ask the question: would it be possible to turn out the light on the world because we've run out of electricity?

Five Star Assembly ✪✪✪✪✪

There are numerous case studies for and against wind farms on the Internet. These could be used to fully immerse the children in the arguments of the debate. They could even take one of the case studies and write and prepare speeches that they could deliver at an imaginary public meeting – perhaps two contrasting speeches, for and against, could be incorporated into the assembly. The children could then take a vote on whether the development should go ahead. Finally, they could create their own news stories based on the outcome, which could also be presented.

24.

Is it Fair Play for Footballers to Cheat?

Three Star Assembly

Themes: Fair play, footballers as role models

Timing: General but could be used to coincide with a significant football tournament or match or if issues arise on the playground

Script

Football is played in small, scruffy corners and huge stadiums all over the world. There are many players with great skill and it is often described as the 'beautiful game'. However, sometimes footballers throw themselves to the ground to try to claim a penalty. On other occasions they will seek to get an opposition player sent off. They may sometimes hurt another player or deliberately commit a foul in order to stop the opposition winning. It is almost as if they want to win at all costs, even if it involves deception. Often footballers are good role models, but on these occasions they are bad role models.

Listen to the following story, which, I am assured, is a true story about a junior football team!

Story

It has to be said that the Crags Hill Under-11 football team were not very good and, furthermore, despite all the practice they seemed to be getting worse. They hadn't won a game all season. In August and September they were losing games by 2-0 and 3-0. However, it was now January and they were losing by 6-0 and 7-0. They enjoyed playing football but were well and truly stuck at the bottom of the table. The only thing they had won all season was an award for being the most sporting team in the league because they always played fairly and never got into trouble with the referee. There was one occasion when a player had actually told the referee that he had fallen down and hadn't been tripped over by an opponent, and as a consequence they forfeited a penalty.

On one Sunday morning, after yet another defeat, they were sat in the wooden hut that was their changing room and they started to wonder if they would ever score a goal or draw a match, let alone win one. They even wondered if they should pack it all in and start to play a different game that they were better at. It was at this point that their manager said, 'Look, I have an idea. We will have an extra training session on Wednesday night but before that I need you all to give me your football boots. I need to look at them and I will clean them for you.' They thought that their manager had gone barmy but they all handed over their boots.

When the boys arrived at the training session on Wednesday night, the coach arrived with a brand new football under his arm and their boots were shining and bright. The boys sat on benches when they were instructed to do so and the coach said, 'Listen carefully, I have something to tell you. Inside each of your football boots there is now a little magnetic radio receiver that gives out electronic diode interdirectory pulses.'

'Electronic diode interdirectory pulses!' the team all said in amazed unison. 'Never heard of them,' retorted Ali, looking straight at his coach.

The manager continued: 'It's based on similar technology to the Nintendo Wii. The football also has a tiny receiver and when you pass the ball to each other it will zip along the ground from one person to another and the opposition will never be able to get near it. Now, let's get changed and see if it works. This will be the ball we'll use for Sunday's match against Glen Green Rovers.' This was the game they had been dreading all season. Glen Green Rovers were top of the league by some distance.

The team changed and went out to try the new ball. They were wearing their shiny boots and one of the boys said, 'The pulses are making my feet tingle, will I be alright?' 'You'll be fine,' said the coach. Within seconds more members of the team said that their feet were tingling too. But when they started to practise they found that the ball did zip along the grass just as the manager had predicted. The team found that they had to run quicker and even think quicker because the ball seemed to move that much faster. However, every pass was true and went straight from the feet of one player to those of a teammate, who then dribbled and twisted and turned before passing the ball on to another player. It was like magic. The team said their feet felt light and never once did the ball go out of their control.

It was just the same during the big match with Glen Green Rovers on the Sunday. A big crowd had gathered and there was a rumour that there were scouts from some of the professional teams in the Football League present who had come to see just how good Glen Green Rovers were. The crowd were highly impressed – not by the team at the top of the league but the one rooted at the bottom that hadn't scored a goal in seven weeks. They passed the ball and it whizzed over the grass from player to player. Before long the team was building up sequences of ten, fifteen and even twenty passes. The spectators on the touchline started to cheer every time a pass was completed. Glen Green Rovers huffed and puffed but they were always chasing shadows. By half-time they were losing 2-0. In the second half, Crags Hill just got better and better, and by the last ten minutes they had a comfortable 3-0 lead and were playing exhibition football. At one stage they built up a sequence of twenty-seven passes.

At the end of the game, they punched the air and listened to the applause from the crowd. They knew that they had given Glen Green Rovers a real football lesson and entertained the crowd at the same time. They were elated as they trooped back into the changing rooms and conversation and chatter filled the air. However, Ali remained quiet and instead of being pleased he seemed extremely sad. Eventually Josh turned around and said, 'What's the matter with you, Ali? We've just beaten the team at the top of the league 3-0!' Ali looked up and simply said, 'But we cheated and we all know it.' The room fell silent as the team turned to hear what Ali would say next.

'Look, we all know we won because of the radio transmitters in our boots and in the ball. Without those you all know we would have probably lost 10-0 again. We weren't good at playing football; the transmitters were good at doing their job.' The changing room fell silent again as the team realized they had won a game by cheating. There was no longer a sense of celebration. Then Ali stood up and announced that he was going to tell the referee what had happened.

The manager spoke next. 'There is no need for that,' he said. 'There were no transmitters in your boots or in the ball. I just wanted you to believe there was, and I wanted you to believe that when you passed the ball it would go straight to a teammate. I wanted you to believe that you could win a game of football. You *are* a good team but you didn't have any belief in yourselves.'

'But what about the electronic diode interdirectory pulses?' asked Ali.

'Never heard of them,' said the manager.

Questions to consider:

- Do you think it feels good when you win honestly?

- Does it feel good when you win dishonestly?

- How does it feel when you lose a game because the opposition has cheated?

- Did the manager do the right thing in tricking the team?

- How important is confidence when you play sport?

- When are footballers good role models and when are they poor role models?

Four Star Assembly ✪ ✪ ✪ ✪

In many of the major football competitions the teams enter behind a flag saying 'Fair Play'. The organization that runs football, the International Federation of Association Football (FIFA), has a definition of what constitutes fair play. Here are some of the elements:

1. Play to win but accept defeat with dignity.

2. Observe the laws of the game.

3. Respect opponents, teammates, referees, officials and spectators.

4. Promote the interests of football.

5. Honour those who defend football's good reputation.

6. Denounce those who attempt to discredit the sport.

> You could display these principles and ask the children which of them were evident in the story. You could also open up a debate about whether teams who stick to these principles should be rewarded.

> Leaving the list on display, you could then move on to two additional stories.

Script

In the Premier League season of 2011/12 there were two contrasting incidents that relate to the fair play guidance.
On two occasions during the season, players were accused of racially insulting a member of the opposing team. In other words, they were suggesting that a player was a lesser person because of the colour of his skin.

In one instance, a player refused to shake hands with a member of the opposition prior to a game because of a racist incident that had previously been investigated. On these occasions the players were not good role models, but I wonder if you can identify which rules within the Fair Play code of conduct were broken?

In 2012, Tottenham Hotspur was playing against Bolton Wanderers in front of a huge crowd. All of a sudden a Bolton player called Fabrice Muamba collapsed. The crowd quickly fell silent. They knew that something was seriously wrong. A doctor who was a specialist in cardiac arrest was in the crowd. He recognized immediately what had happened and went to join the medical team on the pitch. A lengthy period of treatment followed. Many feared that the player would die. Eventually the

player was moved to an ambulance and rushed to hospital. The referee blew his whistle to abandon the game. The ball would not be kicked again during the afternoon and the crowd quietly left the stadium.

Over the next few days, Fabrice Muamba received cards and good wishes, not just from the Bolton Wanderers' supporters, but also from footballers and fans from all over the world. Hundreds of people came to the Bolton Wanderers football ground to leave flowers and scarves. Which of the rules within the code of conduct were evident on this occasion?

Five Star Assembly ⭐⭐⭐⭐⭐

There are many examples of genuine fair play in professional football. The children could research them prior to the assembly and present their findings.

Alternatively, here is another example about which you could ask the children for their response. Midfielder Morten Wieghorst deliberately missed a penalty kick while captaining Denmark against Iran at a Carlsberg Cup match in 2003. Thinking he had heard the referee whistle for half-time, an Iranian defender picked up the ball inside his penalty area; unfortunately the whistle had come from the stands. 'It was unfair to capitalize on that,' said Wieghorst, who subsequently consulted with his coach Morten Olsen before firing wide. Denmark subsequently lost 1-0. However, Wieghorst picked up an Olympic Committee fair play award. He said he preferred this to winning dishonestly.

25.
An Olympic Legacy

Three Star Assembly ✪✪✪

Script

Take a look at the image of the five Olympic rings. The photograph was taken in a London railway station. Do you think you can name the year and do you know what is special about the colours of the rings?

In 2012, sportsmen and women from all around the world descended on London to take part in the Olympic Games. The Olympic flag – which consists of five concentric rings – flew high above the stadium. The flag was designed by the father of the modern Olympic Games. He was called Pierre de Coubertin and the flag has flown at every Olympic Games since 1920. The flag is designed in a very clever way and tells the story of the Olympic movement, which is about much more than just sport.

Story

Pierre de Coubertin was a Frenchman who came up with the idea of resurrecting the Olympic Games on a worldwide scale in the 1890s. He looked around at some of the things that were happening in the world. Many soldiers in his home country had lost their lives in damaging wars and he thought that a new form of Olympic Games could help to bring together in unity the different nations and faiths of the world.

He wanted the new Olympic movement to educate all people and not just sportspeople. He designed the Olympic Games to:

+ Promote the balanced development of the mind, body and character.

+ Celebrate the joy to be found in effort and constantly trying to do that little bit better.

+ Use the excellence of the athletes as a good role model to others.

+ Promote tolerance, generosity, unity, friendship, non-discrimination and respect for others.

Maybe Pierre de Coubertin thought the Olympic Games could even bring an end to war and conflict.

So why is the Olympic flag so cleverly designed? Pierre de Coubertin knew he had to create a flag that was liked by all the nations and faiths in the world. The five interlocking rings represent each of the five great continents that participate in the Olympic Games (Europe, Asia, North America, South America and Oceania). They are linked to signify that athletes from all over the world have come together to compete within a spirit of friendship. Each of the five rings is a different colour (blue, black, red, yellow and green) and the background to the flag is white. However, not only does each colour represent a particular continent, but if you take the five colours and the white background you have at least one of the colours from the flag of every competing nation.

A key part of Pierre de Coubertin's dream was to make the world a friendlier place where people would respect and understand each other. So, have the 2012 Olympic Games left us with a legacy of understanding?

Questions to consider:

■ Can you think of three ways in school that we show friendship and care for one another?

■ Can you think of some good sporting role models to follow?

■ Who thinks that day-by-day they perform that little bit better?

■ Can we think of places in our community, or elsewhere in the country or the world, where people need to spend more time understanding each other and working together?

From these discussions you could also consider whether the Olympic ideals would make the foundation for a good set of school rules.

Four Star Assembly ✪✪✪✪

Instead of telling the children how the colours of the Olympic flag relate to all the countries of the world, you could show them images of national flags and ask if they can spot one that does not include the Olympic colours.

If there is time to work with a group of children before the assembly, you could point out that sometimes in the past countries have been banned from attending the Olympics and at other times nations haven't wanted to compete because their 'enemies' are taking part. You could discuss with them whether this does good or is damaging. The children's views could be reflected in the assembly.

Another way of extending the story might be to tell the story of Eddie 'The Eagle' Edwards and ask which of the Olympic ideals he met.

Story

Eddie was born in Cheltenham and through hard work became a good downhill skier. He had an ambition to compete in the Olympic Games but he also knew this was unlikely to happen because there were other British skiers who were even better than him. So, to improve his chances of qualifying for the 1988 Winter Olympics, he decided to take up ski jumping. This was because there were no other British ski jumpers likely to enter and this would ensure he became Britain's sole entry.

While Eddie was deadly serious in his dream, there are many parts of his story that are quite comic. At the start he didn't have the right equipment and he'd never tried ski jumping or received any training. So, first of all he borrowed some equipment, but as the boots were too big he had to wear six pairs of socks to make them fit. Eddie was also farsighted which meant that he always had to wear his glasses when he jumped, but he found that they steamed up when he put his helmet on and this meant he could

barely see where he was going. To make things worse, he was frightened of heights. He was always worried that his next jump might be his last. He hoped an ambulance was always nearby.

He trained hard but soon ran out of funds and was working at a hospital when he heard the news that he would be the only representative for Great Britain in the ski jumping at the 1988 Winter Olympics. His dream of participating in the Olympics had come true through hard work and overcoming difficulties. However, he wasn't very good compared to the other ski jumpers in the competition. One journalist said that he wasn't a ski jumper, he was a 'ski dropper'. Unfortunately, Eddie came last in both the events he took part in. However, it was not all bad news because he did set a British record of 73.5 metres during the games – and the crowds loved him and watching him fly through the air (well, sort of fly), nicknaming him Eddie the Eagle.

Five Star Assembly ⭐⭐⭐⭐⭐

You could conclude the assembly by returning to the Olympic ideals, which are reflected in Pierre de Coubertin's creed:

The most important thing in the Olympic Games is not to win but to take part, just as the most important thing in life is not the triumph but the struggle. The essential thing is not to have conquered but to have fought well. The Film *Cool Runnings* tells the almost true story of the Jamaican bobsleigh team.

An extract from this film could be used to demonstrate this point. The opening and closing ceremonies of the Olympic Games are a marvellous celebration of how the nations come together in friendship. The use of film footage could enhance the assembly further.

26.
First Amongst Unequals:
England's First Black Footballer

Three Star Assembly ●●●

Script

Take a look at the image. It shows a photograph of a boy trying to peer through a gap in the wall to watch a football match. The photograph was taken in Africa. Sport should bring together in harmony people from over the world to take part in games and competition. Many football stadiums have giant posters saying 'Football unites, racism divides'. Sometimes it doesn't seem to work this way. Fortunately, very few people experience extreme racial hatred. However, this is the story of a young man who did and at a time of his life that should have been very special to him. The man in the story had a dream and he went on to fulfil it. Viv Anderson was the first black footballer to play for England, but his story could have been very different.

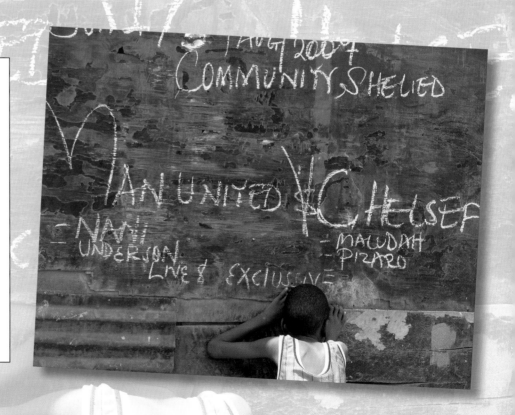

AUG 2004
COMMUNITY SHELIED
MAN UNITED V CHELSEA
- NANI
- UNDERSON
- MALUDAH
- PIZARO
LIVE & EXCLUSIVE

Story

Early in his career, Viv Anderson played for Nottingham Forest. He was still a teenager during the 1970s and this should have been an exciting time for him. Things were changing quickly for Viv: instead of playing for the juniors and reserve teams in stadiums that were virtually empty, he was now on the verge of playing for the first team. His constant hard work and practice was about to take him to some of the finest football grounds in the country and this meant that he would also play against some of the country's best teams and players.

During these early days he had to travel to the north-east of England to play in an important cup game. In his autobiography, *First Amongst Unequals*, he tells the story of running out onto the pitch before the game to warm up, only to be taunted by thousands of supporters chanting racist abuse and throwing things at him. He was experiencing extreme hatred because of the colour of his skin. The noise from the crowd was deafening. It was as though thousands of people were shouting abuse at him at the tops of their voices. He started to feel sick. Viv Anderson says he just froze and then fear struck. He left the pitch and told his manager that he didn't want to play. The young Viv could have walked out of the football stadium that day and never kicked a football again.

Nobody can be certain what was said next, but instead of walking away he dug deep into his personal strength and returned to the pitch. At one stage during the match, he was pushed and crashed into the cinder track and advertising hoardings that surrounded the pitch. He was left cut, bleeding and bruised, and once more the fans jeered as a way of expressing their hatred.

I'm sure this was not Viv Anderson's first experience of racism. His father had arrived in England from Jamaica in 1954 and had secured work as a hospital porter. He was part of the first great wave of immigration from the West Indies. At that stage, it was not uncommon for boarding houses to have signs saying 'no blacks'. However, nothing compared to what he experienced that night in Newcastle.

Viv Anderson knew that he needed to be strong. Many young boys dream of being a professional footballer and he was no different. He was determined to live his dream. On weekdays he practised and trained hard for matches. However, week after week he ran out onto the pitch only to hear more racist abuse. After a time, Viv managed to block it out and he simply focused on being the best footballer he could be. Week by week and month by month he got stronger and played better until on 27 November 1978, he heard that he had been selected to play in the white shirt of England. He would walk proudly onto the pitch to be cheered by 100,000 spectators. This would be so different from those early days when he had suffered such abuse.

Viv Anderson would play for England on a further thirty occasions over the following years. But I wonder what would have happened to him had he walked out of that football stadium all those years before and never returned?

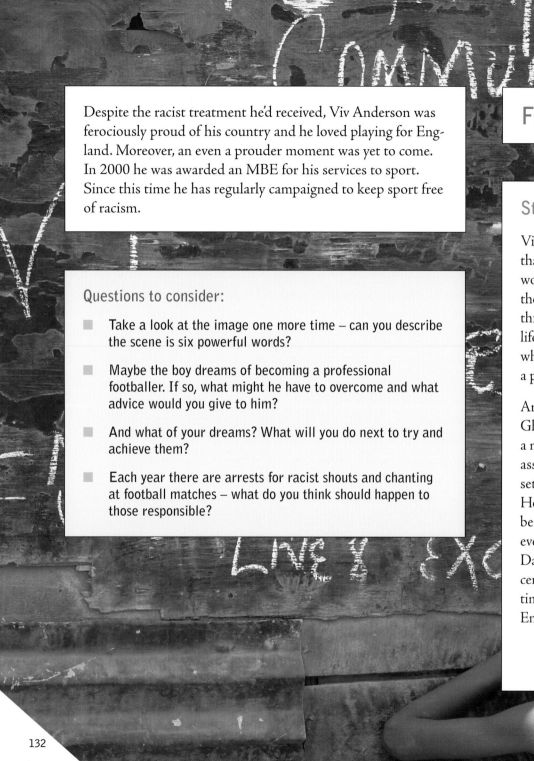

Despite the racist treatment he'd received, Viv Anderson was ferociously proud of his country and he loved playing for England. Moreover, an even a prouder moment was yet to come. In 2000 he was awarded an MBE for his services to sport. Since this time he has regularly campaigned to keep sport free of racism.

Questions to consider:

- Take a look at the image one more time – can you describe the scene is six powerful words?

- Maybe the boy dreams of becoming a professional footballer. If so, what might he have to overcome and what advice would you give to him?

- And what of your dreams? What will you do next to try and achieve them?

- Each year there are arrests for racist shouts and chanting at football matches – what do you think should happen to those responsible?

Four Star Assembly ✪✪✪✪

Story

Viv Anderson was not really the 'First Amongst Unequals' – that claim to fame lies elsewhere. The ideal follow-up assembly would relate to the first ever black professional footballer in the world. He was called Arthur Wharton. You could start this part of the assembly by asking the question: I wonder if life would have been different for Arthur Wharton if he'd been white? His story is readily available on the Internet, but here is a précis.

Arthur Wharton was born in Jamestown, Gold Coast (now Ghana), in 1865 and his life story is amazing. His mother was a member of the Fante Akan royal family and therefore we can assume that he came from a wealthy background. In 1882 he set sail for England in order to train as a Methodist preacher. However, Arthur quickly decided that there was more fun to be had within the world of sport. He was signed as the first ever black professional footballer in the UK when he joined Darlington Football Club, where he was described as 'magnificent' and 'superb'. He later played for Preston North End at a time when they were described as the most invincible team in England.

However, it was not just football and goalkeeping that Arthur Wharton excelled at. He also set a record time for cycling between Preston and Blackburn and, in 1886, he became the fastest man in the world when he became the first person to run a hundred yards in just ten seconds.

Arthur Wharton then moved to Rotherham United where he played for six years. During his career he suffered extreme racism, not just from spectators but from the newspapers as well. However, Arthur was a proud man who was determined to show people that he was as good as any white player, and often better. As a result he sometimes did very strange things. One newspaper reporter wrote: 'In a match between Rotherham and Sheffield Wednesday at Olive Grove I saw Wharton jump, take hold of the cross bar, catch the ball between his legs and cause three onrushing forwards … to fall into the net. I have never seen a similar save since and I have been watching football for over fifty years.'

Arthur Wharton never returned to Gold Coast. His family had disowned him when he took up sport, which they thought was inappropriate. When his sporting career was over, he went to work as a coal miner near Doncaster and he spent his last years in a sanatorium before being buried as a pauper in an unmarked grave. Many people have been left to wonder if this fabulously talented sportsman would have had a different life story if his skin had been white.

The story of Arthur Wharton has recently had a happier ending. Many people have worked to make sure his legacy is remembered. A new headstone was provided for his grave in 1997 which acknowledges his significant achievements. A statue of him was presented to the president of FIFA in 2012 and it will remain on permanent display at their headquarters.

The story of Arthur Wharton and the challenges he faced can also be found in several short films available on the Internet. These could enhance the learning activity further.

Five Star Assembly ⭐⭐⭐⭐⭐

Story

There is a third story that could be used to extend the assembly even further. Alice Coachman overcame adversity to become the first female African-American to win a gold medal at the Olympic Games. Alice was born in 1923 in Albany in the southern states of America, and she was one of ten children. In this part of the world, black athletes were not allowed to use any of the training facilities or compete in organized sports events due to the strict segregation that existed at the time. There was also a great deal of opposition to women competing in sports. However, Alice loved to sprint and jump and so she trained wherever she could. If that meant running barefoot through fields or on dust tracks, then that is what she did. She improvised with home-made equipment to make high jump stands, using ropes, sticks and rags that were tied together.

Alice's parents tried hard to discourage her. They wanted her to take part in more 'ladylike' activities. However, Alice had the help of an aunt, who helped her to fulfil her dream. In 1939, she managed to gain entry into the Women's National Championships where she broke the national high jump record. This was even more remarkable because she did it barefoot.

Alice continued to train and work hard. In 1948, she went to the Olympic Games in London where she won a gold medal in front of a huge audience. The people back home in Albany watched Alice win her medal and, for the first time ever, the town held a parade to salute the achievements of a black person. The mayor congratulated her on her achievements – but refused to shake her hand!

27.

An Englishman's Home May Be His Castle, but It Isn't Very English

Three Star Assembly ⭐⭐⭐

Script

This image shows a typical living room in the 1940s. How is this different to our living rooms at home today. There is an old saying that an Englishman's home is his castle, which suggests that when he is at home he will be warm, comfortable and safe from danger. The next story is about George who came home to his castle.

Story

George entered his home after an early morning stroll. He loved coming home. It was full of his most treasured possessions and he had worked hard to make it a very special place. He slipped off his very comfortable, aerodynamically designed Malaysian made training shoes and put on his stylish Italian slippers. He entered his Scandinavian designed kitchen and sat down to enjoy his favourite breakfast of chilled Spanish orange juice and cornflakes made from Hungarian maize. To add a little more flavour, he sliced up a tasty Jamaican banana. He finished the meal with some Columbian coffee, which he drank from a cup that was made in Taiwan.

After that he went into his living room and sat on his Swedish sofa. He picked up the TV remote control to switch to the test match from Australia on his Korean television, which was connected to his DVD player that was made in Singapore. The signal on the high-definition screen came through loud and clear, beamed from a satellite somewhere in outer space, which was put there by a US spaceship. He sank into his soft and luxurious Turkish cushions ready to be entertained. As the programme switched to the adverts George looked out of the window and thought he must remember to wash his highly reliable German car this weekend.

As lunch approached, his wife called him through to the kitchen to enjoy a meal of tasty New Zealand lamb, fresh Egyptian potatoes topped with Danish butter and vegetables from Guatemala and Mexico. He was sat on a comfortable chair at a matching wooden table, both made in Finland. He finished his dinner with some Kenyan tea and a piece of Belgian chocolate. He then helped to load the dishes into the Japanese dishwasher and added the appropriate detergent tablets, which were made in France.

Now the strange thing about this story is that you can choose what happens next. Which do you think is the better ending?

After lunch George left the dining room, carefully opening and closing the door made of Norwegian wood, and walked across the Iranian carpet and switched on his Apple computer, which was made in China. He then realized that the battery was running low, so he went and got the Indonesian manufactured lead and connected it to the Indian made socket. As the screen of his high-resolution Vietnamese monitor came to life he scanned the news articles, which included the use of cheap labour in overcrowded factories in Pakistan, children being forced to miss school in order to work on coffee plantations in Africa and how conflict in the Middle East could affect oil supplies. George scratched his chin and said, 'I don't want anything to do with those foreigners – you can't rely on them!'

Or:

After lunch George left the dining room, carefully opening and closing the door made of Norwegian wood, and walked across the Iranian carpet and switched on his Apple computer, which was made in China. He then realized that the battery was running low, so he went and got the Indonesian manufactured lead and connected it to the Indian made socket. As the screen of his high-resolution Vietnamese monitor came to life he read the very story we are reading now, because somebody had emailed it to him. And George started to think, wow, how many people's hands have helped to create the wonderful things in this house. Wouldn't it be marvellous if those people from all around the world could come together, hold hands and speak to each other, and then I could say thank you to them for helping to create my perfect home.

Questions to consider:

■ Take another look at the image – where do you think the furniture in the picture was made?

■ Today many of the things in our homes are made overseas. What are the advantages and disadvantages of this?

Five Star Assembly ⭐⭐⭐⭐⭐

As a further extension to the activity, you could track down the origins of some of the products and fittings in your school. You could take photographs of them in use and then locate the factories where they were originally produced. You could send your pictures to the factory and try to find out more about how the products were made and the standard of living of the workers.

Four Star Assembly ⭐⭐⭐⭐

Prior to the assembly, ask a group of children to find ten products made in ten different countries in their home. You could also track the distances travelled by these items into their homes. The information could be presented in various ways during the assembly – for example, the children could bring in a world map with lines linking the country of origin with their home, or they could make a list of the items with the distance they had travelled. It may be possible to group the items to see if electrical items come from a particular part of the world, or which continents we rely most on for food.

Another interesting option might be to take a complex electronic device, like a mobile phone, and identify the components (antenna, circuit board, microphone/speaker, battery, etc.), and then find out where they come from and how they are made. For example, Coltan, which is used in tantalum capacitors in circuit boards, is mined under terrible conditions in eastern Congo by miners paid meagre wages and in mines controlled by armed militias. Perhaps the learners could also consider what happens to consumer devices when we later throw them away.

Stornoway Gazette

AUGUST 1955
1 2 3 4 5 6

28.

Someone Who Thinks the World is Always Cheating Him is Right: Choose Your Attitude

Three Star Assembly ⭐ ⭐ ⭐

Script

Take a look at the image, especially the sign that says 'no grumpy people allowed'. How does it make you feel? Would you want to enter the shop – it sounds like it might be fun? Every day we choose our attitude, and it is generally believed that those who are positive live far happier lives and have more fun.

Story

It was 8.30 a.m. and Jackie opened her front door at exactly the same time as her next-door neighbour Peter. Each morning they went for a walk that consisted of almost the same route – they just chose to walk it in opposite directions and with totally different attitudes. Jackie came out of the house and turned left and Peter chose to turn right. Jackie had often suggested that they did the walk together and keep each other company, but she never found Peter to be good company. Just as each person chose which route to take, they also decided the mood and attitude they would take with them. Jackie tended to be an optimist and looked on the bright side of life. Peter was more of a pessimist and always seemed surrounded with problems.

Peter looked grumpy as he turned out onto the high street and let out a deep sigh as the little man turned from green to red on the pelican crossing. It always seemed to do that and he hated standing around. As he crossed the road and started to walk past the row of restaurants he moaned again. He looked at the shopfronts and muttered under his breath, 'An Indian restaurant, an Italian restaurant, a Chinese restaurant, a Thai restaurant and finally a New York Hamburger bar. I don't know what this street is coming to any longer. I remember when they all used to be proper shops like haberdashers, milliners and ironmongers. That's what we need – proper shops!' The truth is that these shops had all closed down long ago because people, including Peter, had stopped shopping there.

As he moved further down the high street, he came to a large shop that was in two distinctive halves. The sign above spread over both sides and said 'Kashmir Stores'. An Asian family who had arrived in the country twenty years ago owned this shop. One side contained delicate and brightly coloured fabrics in every shade imaginable for making into fine clothes. The other half of the shop sold fresh fruit and vegetables. Every day the owner, Mr Sharma, could be seen building up a tremendous display of his goods on improvised tables that seemed to bend under the weight of produce. Mr Sharma said good morning to Peter, just as he did to any passer-by. However, Peter just buried his hands deeper into his pockets and moved quickly past in the direction of the Polish mini-market.

Finally, he passed the doctor's surgery and noticed the brass nameplate, which read 'Dr Patel'. Peter had attended this surgery for many years but had stopped using it when the new doctor had arrived a couple of years back. He told his neighbours that he didn't like the new GP because he wasn't as good as Dr Simpson. From this point he headed home.

As always Jackie set off at the same time, but she moved in the opposite direction and so the first landmark he passed by was the doctor's. As she went by the surgery she paused and thought, as she always did, that she owed a great debt towards Dr Patel. Jackie had been suffering with severe chest pains and had called the doctor in the middle of the night. She had never felt so ill before and had been really frightened. The doctor had come immediately and quickly diagnosed a heart problem. Dr Patel went all the way to hospital with her just in case her condition deteriorated on the way.

As Jackie moved from the doctor's, she passed the Polish mini-market and the owner Mr Marcinkiewicz was just coming out. She loved talking to him. Mr Marcinkiewicz's grandfather had flown alongside British pilots during the Second World War and had been awarded a military medal for completing a particular mission and landing his aircraft safely even though seriously wounded. He had been losing blood and had landed with just minutes to spare. Jackie thought it was sad that people hadn't welcomed Mr Marcinkiewicz to the area given that his father was a war hero. Some people had said, 'We don't need a Polish supermarket around here'. This reminded Jackie of her own grandfather who had arrived in Britain from Ireland at the start of the Second World War. He too had wanted to help the war effort by working in the steel works to make munitions. Despite the fact he had come to help, the lodging houses had signs in them saying 'No Irish'.

As Jackie moved on, someone in a car blew his horn at her. She turned around to see a taxi driven by her friend Asif. He waved vigorously to Jackie. The two of them had become close friends over the years. Jackie loved watching cricket and they often went to watch matches together. Outside Kashmir Stores, Mr Sharma was still building up his display of fruit and vegetables. As Jackie approached he said hello to Jackie in the same friendly way that he'd greeted Peter. The difference was that Jackie stopped and spoke with him for several minutes before continuing on her journey.

As she passed the restaurants and takeaways, the wonderful aroma of food was already in the air. Jackie had eaten in all of the restaurants on many occasions. She loved all of them and liked nothing better than to ask the chef or owner which dish they would recommend if she wanted to get the authentic taste of that country or region.

Jackie continued on her journey home and arrived home smiling. She looked across at Peter who was just unlocking his own door. He looked sad and grumpy. Jackie wondered if Peter would have been any happier if he'd chosen to turn left instead of right. What do you think might have made Peter feel happier?

Now pause and ask the children what words they would use to describe Jackie and Rob. You could use a flip chart and make a table like the one below.

Words to describe Peter	Words to describe Jackie

Questions to consider:

- Which person, out of Peter and Jackie, do you think is the happiest in life?

- Which person, out of Peter and Jackie, would you be more likely to help or be friends with?

- What words would you use to describe Jackie's personality?

- How would you describe Peter? Was he being fair to the people around him or was there evidence of racism and prejudice? How does his behaviour make you feel?

Five Star Assembly ⭐⭐⭐⭐⭐

Many people who live in the UK have forebears from other nations. You could ask a class of children to aid you with some research for this assembly by asking them to track down the origins of their parents and grandparents. This is another way of showing how people of different nationalities, faiths and cultures come together to make Britain a wonderful and diverse place to live.

You could also consider closing the assembly with a famous quote from Eric Hoffer: 'Someone who thinks the world is always cheating him is right. He is missing that wonderful feeling of trust in someone or something.'

Four Star Assembly ⭐⭐⭐⭐

The UK is a very multicultural nation. Use the time before the assembly to work with the children to look for examples of other cultures and faiths in your community. This could be reflected on a map drawn by the children. Alternatively, pupils could produce their own story of a walk around their local area based on Jackie's trip.

29.

And Today's Lesson Comes from the Arctic Monkeys

Three Star Assembly ★★★

Script

Technology is constantly changing our lives and we constantly need to adapt and change if we are going to be successful in life. During the early years of the twenty-first century, some of the biggest shops disappeared from the high street because they failed to move with the times. Here comes a success story about a group of people who did adapt and change, and reached their dream by doing things differently.

Story

In the summer of 2013, the Arctic Monkeys played to a huge audience at the Glastonbury Music Festival and to millions of people who tuned in around the world on their radios, televisions and computers. The band play to packed audiences in arenas and stadiums all around the world. Their recording contracts are worth millions of pounds. When they play in front of six-figure audiences they must feel like superstars, and those looking up at them believe they are superstars as they cheer and join in with the lyrics of their favourite songs. The band creates an electric atmosphere. However, for them it was not the quick stardom of *The X-Factor* or a television talent show watched by millions of viewers texting in their votes. So, how did they achieve their fame?

1. *They had a dream.* The Arctic Monkeys were a group of lads who loved making music and had a dream. The band was their passion and playing music and singing was what they had always wanted to do.

2. *They created their own luck.* Sometimes people are very suspicious of those who become successful. They say they just experienced a bit of luck along the way. Occasionally people are lucky – for example, they might win a big prize in a lottery. The Arctic Monkeys didn't just get lucky though; they made their own luck, which is what most successful people do. But how do people make their own luck? Usually the way in which people create their own luck is through hard work. And the way in which the Arctic Monkeys did it was through constantly practising and changing and adapting the music and words in their songs until they were perfect. A famous golfer once said, 'The more I practise the luckier I get'. A famous violinist once said, 'I practised for 10,000 hours and now they call me a genius!' The Arctic Monkeys practised and practised and then started to create their own lucky breaks. But to do this they had to make the most of their circumstances and environment.

3. *They made the most of the location they were in.* The band didn't rehearse in luxurious surroundings. They used a little back-street building in an area of Sheffield called Neepsend which was surrounded by old factories. There were lots of small public houses in the area where new bands could play and so, when they weren't practising, they played for virtually no money in local pubs, and after each performance they sat down and considered how they could improve.

4. *They made the most of the time they were in and were generous to others.* The Arctic Monkeys knew that they had to make the most of the time that they lived in, and the period at the start of the twenty-first century was a rapidly changing technological world. It suddenly became easier to record and copy music. And so the band started making their own CDs – not to sell, but to give away. At the end of one of their performances, they would simply hand out their CDs to anybody in the audience who wanted one. However, the band was becoming so good that other people started copying the CDs and passing them on, and this helped their reputation to spread further. Then, before long, their fans started putting their music onto the Internet, allowing their fame to develop even more.

The Arctic Monkeys then started to think very seriously about their first professional recording. They decided to create their own recording label and sell their music solely on the Internet for download. This would remove the need for a lot of 'middle men' who make, package and distribute CDs as well as the shopkeepers who sell them. Eventually they signed a recording contract with Domino and released their single 'I Bet You Look Good on the Dancefloor'. It quickly started selling more copies than Robbie Williams and became the first record to reach number one in the UK charts with virtually no marketing or advertising.

From that point on, The Arctic Monkeys have gone from strength to strength. Their first album is the fastest-selling debut album for a British band. There are always lots of teachers in schools who are ready to offer advice, but just for today let's forget them and take a lesson from the Arctic monkeys by considering what they did:

1. Have passion.

2. Work hard to create your own luck.

3. Make the most of the location you are in.

4. Make the most of the time you are in.

Questions to consider:

- Ask the children about the dreams they have and using the model above, ask the others to offer guidance on what they may need to do to turn the dream into a reality.

Four Star Assembly ✪ ✪ ✪ ✪

Ask the children to reflect on when they have made their own luck, either through working hard to achieve a breakthrough or a particular moment of success, or when being generous to others has led to good fortune at a later stage.

You could create a table on a flip chart to record this like the one below:

Name	How he/she worked hard	The outcome	How he/she was generous to others	The outcome

Five Star Assembly ⭐⭐⭐⭐⭐

There is research that shows that the pattern above runs fairly accurately for most people who become highly successful. If you wish to take the assembly further, you could get the children to research the life stories of other famous people, or some of their favourite role models, or speak to people who have been particularly high achievers, and see how closely it matches the recipe for success.

If the children are going to interview people, the types of questions they need to ask are:

• When did you develop a passion for your work?

• In what ways did you work hard?

• How did you make good use of your surroundings?

• In what ways were the times you were living in important?

The children could design a PowerPoint presentation or video relating to their role model using the headings above. These could be shown in a subsequent assembly.

Part II

Creating Responsible
Citizens in Our Schools
and Communities

Promoting a sense of aspiration and ambition within learners
and also providing ideas for how they can make a positive
difference to the school and the locality.

30.
The Mathematics of the Widow's Mite

Three Star Assembly ⭐ ⭐ ⭐

There is a common misconception that all the major faiths in the world are very different and that this sometimes leads to argument and conflict. The truth is that they also have many similarities and there is often more that unites them than divides them. This assembly seeks to demonstrate this unity.

Start the assembly by asking the children to take a look at the image and consider the question can a twenty pound note ever be worth more than a 20p coin, pointing out that you will return to the question later.

The assembly is based on a famous story from the Bible (Luke 21:1–4). It is called the Lesson of the Widow's Mite.

Story

One day Jesus was in the temple and talking to his followers who were gathered around him. They wanted to listen and learn from him because they hoped to become better people. The Jews were expected to give money to the temple and also to the poor as part of their service to God. Jesus asked his followers to watch how people were putting money into the collection box.

The disciples carefully observed what was going on, and they saw that people not only gave different amounts of money but they also made their gift in various ways. Some of the richer traders and businessmen showed off and waited until they knew a lot of people were watching and then donated a large amount of money. These individuals thought they were the centre of attention and that others would speak well of their considerable generosity. Other people looked unhappy as though they really didn't want to give any of their money away.

One rich merchant came forward first. He owned 1,000 gold coins. He was wearing a beautiful golden cloak and made an elaborate sweep of his arm when he gave away one gold coin for every hundred that he owned.

Next a trader came forward. He didn't look quite so happy; in fact he looked extremely miserable. He also owned 1,000 gold coins and he put one hundred of them into the collecting box.

The third person to come forward travelled the country selling fine clothes. He also owned 1,000 gold coins and he put two hundred of them into the collection box.

Next the king came forward surrounded by his servants. He was a very rich man who taxed his people heavily. He owned 10,000 gold coins. As he arrived at the collection box he loudly announced that he was going to donate half of his wealth and he challenged everybody else to do the same.

Now this was a serious challenge, and for a while nobody moved towards the collection box. People simply sat and watched, and then an old widow woman, dressed in ragged black clothing, slowly hobbled into the temple. She looked out of place amidst the rich merchants around her. They moved away from her in disgust because they didn't want to be seen alongside poor people. The elderly woman emptied the entire contents of her purse into the collection box. Just two very small coins called mites fell amongst the other coins. The rich people around her made tutting noises of disapproval and looked towards the ceiling.

Equally, the disciples around Jesus were also unimpressed. They said she had given far too little, but Jesus disagreed and said she had given far more than anyone else.

Questions to consider:

- Who do you think gave the most?

- Who do you think gave the least?

- Who was the most generous person in the story?

- Who was the least generous person in the story?

- How could the old woman have given more than the rich merchants and traders?

So what has this story got in common with the other religions? All the major religions suggest that their followers should give money to charity. Here are some key words.

Tithe is an old English word meaning a tenth. Each year Christian people were expected to donate a tenth of their annual income as a tax to support the Church.

Zakat is a word from the Muslim faith. Each year people are expected to donate 2.5% of their income and after the holy month of Ramadan they should donate the price of a meal.

Tzedaka is a Jewish word meaning 'doing the right thing' or 'charitable giving'. Once again, followers of the Jewish faith are encouraged to donate 10% of their annual wealth to charity.

Vedic is the period in which the Hindu faith was laid out. Followers of Hinduism believe they should donate up to 50% of their income to charity and this is a key part the Vedic tradition.

Followers of Buddhism also believe in the notion of taking the 'right actions' with money so that it makes a difference to others.

Finally, the Sikh code of conduct advocates that 10% of income should be given to charity.

Four Star Assembly ★★★★

To add interest at the start of the assembly, have some mathematical fun with money. You could have the full set of British coins and banknotes and ask for a volunteer to arrange them in ascending order. Don't be afraid to add further mathematics into the activity by asking questions such as: What is the total value of the coins (or the total value of the coins and notes)? Then ask the children to work out how the difference in value increases as you go from 1p to 2p to 5p to 10p to 20p and so on. And then finally ask the question: Can our smallest 1p coin ever be worth more than a £20 note?

Alternatively, you could bring an item to the assembly that is a personal possession that cost very little to buy, but is so special that you would never consider selling it. This would also involve telling the children the story of why it has such personal value.

Five Star Assembly ★★★★★

There are many ways in which the assembly could be extended further. You could get children to write and perform their own version of the widow's mite story. These could be put into a modern-day context.

There are also numerous images of the Lesson of the Widow's Mite on the Internet that could be used in the assembly. You could also ask a pupil to read the story from the Bible while displaying the images.

Perhaps you could display the key words relating to the different religions on an interactive whiteboard and ask the children to match them to the appropriate faith.

The widow's mites would have been worthless to one of the rich merchants. He may even have thrown them away. You could extend the assembly by working with a group of children to identify which items they own that are extremely valuable and important to them but would be worthless to someone else. Many of these items will relate to a particular time or event in their lives. The children could bring the items to an assembly and tell the story of their meaning and importance.

31.
Calculating the Value of an Single Egg and the Wisdom of Solomon

Three Star Assembly ⭐ ⭐ ⭐

During the assembly you could use a small Team of Experts with laptop or tablet computers to find other stories based on the Wisdom of Solomon.

Script

There is an old brainteaser about which came first – the chicken or the egg. You may know the answer, but I certainly don't! Here is a twist to that puzzle based on an old Jewish legend about eggs. See if you can work out the meaning behind it. This story also introduces the Wisdom of Solomon.

Story

Once upon a time there was an army and after a hard day of fighting they returned to their base for their evening meal, which consisted of boiled eggs. One of the soldiers was called Adam. After he had eaten his two eggs he still felt very hungry and so he turned to the soldier alongside him, who was called Joshua, and said, 'This is no good, I'm still starving. Can I have one of your boiled eggs?'

Joshua thought about this for a while and said, 'You can't *have* one of my eggs but I will *loan* one of them to you and you can repay me later.'

Adam deliberated hard about this and thought that perhaps Joshua was going a bit barmy. Who lends people boiled eggs and how easy would it be to pay back the egg? Then he thought Joshua would probably forget all about it anyway. Adam's stomach started to rumble again and it reminded him just how hungry he was feeling, so he said, 'Yes, OK, let me have one of your boiled eggs.' The egg was passed over and Adam wolfed it down in seconds.

The two men remained in the army for a long time and Adam forgot all about the egg. However, Joshua didn't forget and one day, after six years, he walked up to Adam and said quite unexpectedly, 'I need to talk to you about the egg you loaned from me.'

'What egg?' asked Adam

Joshua reminded Adam of the day he had been so hungry and had begged him for the extra egg. He angrily finished off by saying, 'Don't you dare pretend you've forgotten about it because today I've come for my payment.'

After a while Adam admitted that he did remember, but sadly said, 'I don't have any eggs, so how can I pay you?'

At that point Joshua said, 'It's not about eggs any longer. It's about money and you now owe me six million gold coins.'

'Don't be ridiculous!' responded Adam crossly. 'I borrowed a boiled egg. How can that mean that I owe you six million gold coins?'

'Well,' replied Joshua, with a glint in his eye, 'if the egg you had eaten had hatched out to become a chicken then in the first year it would have become a hen.

'Then in the second year the hen would have had 20 chickens.

'And then in the next year those 20 chickens would have had 20 more making 400.

'The following year those 400 chickens would have grown into hens and each one would have had 20 chickens making 8,000.

'In the fifth year the 8,000 chickens would have had 20 chickens each and that makes 160,000.

'And this year those 160,000 chickens would have grown into hens and had 20 chickens each making over three million chickens.

'Now, as each chicken is worth two gold coins, you now owe me six million gold coins!'

Adam started to look very frightened because he knew that the honourable thing to do was to pay his debts, but he had only ever expected to pay back one egg. He told Joshua that he needed to go away and think about how he would repay the debt.

As he moved off looking sad and dejected he bumped into Solomon, who was the king's son and deemed to be a very wise man. Solomon looked at Adam and asked, 'Why are you looking so sad? What on earth is the matter?'

Adam explained his problem to Solomon, who then bent over and, very quietly, whispered something into his ear. Adam started to smile because Solomon had helped him to find a solution to the problem. Adam hurried to a nearby field and could soon be seen ploughing it so that it was ready for seeds to be sown. However, what happened next was really quite extraordinary. After he had ploughed the field, Adam started to collect all the cooking pots he could find and then he lit campfires underneath them. Adam started to boil beans. He put hundreds and thousands of beans into the pots and boiled them. After the beans were cooked he then started to carefully plant them in the ploughed field. By now hundreds of people had gathered round to watch Adam, believing he had probably gone mad. Eventually Joshua pushed his way to the front of the crowd.

Joshua shouted to Adam, 'Have you gone mad? What on earth are you doing?'

Adam turned and replied, 'I'm planting beans, which I will sell, and when I have the money I will pay my debt to you.'

'Don't be silly,' snapped Joshua. 'Those beans will never grow. You can't grow plants from beans that have been boiled.'

Adam quickly looked up and said, 'And you can't get chickens from eggs that have been boiled.'

And at that point Joshua knew that he had been beaten and his trick hadn't worked. Adam put down his beans and plough and said, 'Shall we just say that I owe you one boiled egg?'

Questions to consider:

- What do you consider to be the moral of the story?

- What words would you use to describe Joshua and what advice would you give him?

- Can you think of a good title for this story using six powerful words?

- Oh, and which did come first – the chicken or the egg?

If you used the Team of Experts model you could collect their additional information at this point.

Four Star Assembly ★★★★

Prior to telling the story you could widen the children's knowledge and understanding of Judaism. Many schools will have a range of artefacts from different religions, including a model of the Torah, and this could be shown to the children as part of the assembly. The Torah includes the first five books of the Bible and the laws that God wanted the Jewish people to follow. There are 613 commandments in the Torah and they are believed to be God's will.

Followers of the Jewish faith believe that we are all created equal, and that we should care for those who are less fortunate than ourselves and for the environment. Jews believe that people are born with the free will to choose between carrying out acts that are good and acts that are evil. They also believe that the world we have been given is good and plentiful and we have a duty to use it well and to look after it for the benefit of others.

The Jewish tradition includes numerous folk stories and many of them use humour to provoke thought. Lots of them also promote wisdom – particularly the wisdom of Solomon.

Five Star Assembly ★★★★★

You could open the assembly by having fun with the mathematics in the story. Firstly, you could show the children the number 3,200,000 and ask who can say the number in words. Then you could show the children an egg and ask them to imagine that this egg hatches out into a chicken which grows into a hen and has 20 chickens in a year, and then they grow into hens and have 20 chickens in a year. How long do they think it would it be before there are 3,200,000 chickens? Display the calculation on an interactive whiteboard or screen so the children see each stage:

- Year one: 1 x 20

- Year two: 20 x 20

- Year three: 400 x 20

- Year four: 8,000 x 20

- Year five: 160,000 x 20

Only then tell the children you are going to read them a story based on one egg and the calculations they have just used.

32.
Honesty Always Pays

Three Star Assembly ⭐⭐⭐

Script

This shows graffiti sprayed on to a wall saying 'heart shaped mind'. Now listen to this old Islamic folktale. Its messages remain as important today as centuries ago when it was first told. I wonder if you can work out what are the key messages of the story. It may also help you to understand the phrase 'heart shaped mind'.

Story

Once upon a time there was a man who owned a drapers shop. He sold all sorts of wonderful coloured fabrics, threads and buttons. The shop was often full because the people in the village knew that they would get good advice and an honest deal. One day the owner had to leave the shop in the hands of his assistant while he went to see a merchant in order to purchase some new fabrics. Before he left, he told the assistant that all the merchandise in the shop had the right price tickets on them. However, there was a roll of beautiful blue material that had an imperfection in the cloth and therefore had to be sold at half price if anyone wanted to buy it. He made it clear to his assistant that if anybody was interested in buying this fabric they must be shown the defect and instead of selling it for ten gold coins it was to be sold for five gold coins.

After the draper had set off on his journey, a customer came in to buy material to make some new clothes. The assistant asked which colours she was interested in and was told blue. She looked at every roll of blue cloth available but none of them was right, until eventually the defective roll was brought out to her. Instantly, the customer said, 'That is perfect. I absolutely love it and I simply must have it.' The draper's assistant realized the sale was as good as complete and so decided not to offer the reduction and sold it for ten gold coins. He believed the draper would be pleased with him for getting such a good deal.

When the draper returned, the assistant told his story with pride, expecting that he would be praised for his work. However, he quickly realized that he had seriously misjudged the situation. He could see the draper getting more and more angry. 'Why are you so cross?' he asked, 'I thought you would be pleased with me. You've got twice as much money as you were expecting.'

The draper snapped back, 'We have cheated that poor woman and we have been dishonest with her. She believes she has bought perfect material and it is faulty. I have to find her, apologize and offer her money back.'

The assistant said, 'But we don't know where she lives. We will never find her.'

The draper went out into the street and he kept asking people if they knew who might have bought the material. Finally, he found a man who had seen a woman with a roll of blue fabric the day before and he pointed towards her house.

The draper went straight up to the house and knocked on the door. As the woman opened it, the draper began to blurt out his apology and explained that the blue material was faulty. The customer thanked him for his honesty but said she had spotted the fault in the fabric straight away. She also said that she knew she could work around it when she stitched the garment together and therefore there was no need for him to return the five gold coins.

However, the draper was not content. He insisted that the woman had her five gold coins back, because if he didn't return them he would feel like he had stolen them.

Questions to consider:

- The customer was very happy to pay ten gold coins for the material, so was the assistant right to take the money?

- Did the draper do the right thing in returning the money?

- What do you think the customer thought about the draper and is she more likely to return to his shop because he returned her money?

- Does honesty usually pay?

- Now, take another look at the image and consider what a 'heart shaped mind' might mean.

- Can you provide a title for the story using six powerful words?

Four Star Assembly ✪✪✪✪

If time allows, introduce the assembly by taking the opportunity to revise some of the key elements of Islam and discuss the five pillars of the Islamic faith:

- Kalima: the belief in one true God.

- Salat: the duty to pray five times a day.

- Zakat: the need to provide alms for the needy and to good causes.

- Sawm: the requirement to fast between dawn and dusk during the holy month of Ramadan.

- Hajj: the obligation to make a pilgrimage to Mecca at least once during your lifetime.

Muslims believe that Abraham, Noah and Moses were significant prophets, but the most important prophet of all was Muhammad who received revelations that were assembled in the Qur'an. Muslims believe that these are the words of God and that the Qur'an is the most important book in the world.

However, there are many Muslim folktales based on the key principles of the faith including kindness, honesty, forgiveness and humility. This story is one of them.

Five Star Assembly ✪✪✪✪✪

If you have enough time to plan and rehearse, the assembly could be performed as a play. You could tell the story to the children and ask them to write a play script or alternatively you could use the one over the page. The play will be more dramatic if you can use props such as rolls of material and real coins.

The play script

Narrator: Once upon a time there was a man who owned a drapers shop. It sold colourful fabrics, threads and buttons. It was a very popular shop with all those who lived in the area because the customers knew that they would get good advice, and the goods were always sold at very fair prices. One day the shopkeeper had to leave the shop to go away and buy new fabrics. He told his assistant that he would have to look after the shop the next day.

Shopkeeper: Remember, tomorrow I will be away as I have a great deal of travelling to do. I have made sure that you have a full list of all the prices you will need.

Assistant: Yes, Sir, I have the list and I will use it at all times.

Shopkeeper: There is just one thing: you see the roll of blue material over there? It has a fault in it. It is difficult to see but a person who is good at sewing will be able to hide the mark. However, the roll must be sold at half price because it is defective. We must be honest at all times.

Narrator: The shopkeeper left for his travels and the next day the assistant unlocked the shop and was sweeping the floor when the first customer arrived.

Assistant: Good morning and how are you today?

Customer: I am well but I would like to buy some material as I wish to make some new clothes:

Assistant: Do you have a colour in mind?

Customer: Yes, I think I would like blue.

Narrator: The shop assistant showed the customer many rolls of blue fabric; however, none of them were right. Sometimes the blue was the wrong shade, sometimes the cloth was too shiny, sometimes it was too heavy and sometimes it was too light. Eventually there was only one roll of blue material left and that was the one with the mark on it.

Assistant: I'm afraid I have just one more roll to show you and here it is.

Customer: But this is just right. It is exactly what I am looking for. It is the most beautiful shade of blue and the fabric is so soft. The material is perfect. Why did you wait so long to show it to me?

Narrator: Of course, the assistant knew the material was not perfect, but the customer thought it was so he decided to sell it at the full price rather than half price. He thought that the shopkeeper would be pleased with him and possibly give him some extra money that week.

Customer: How much does the fabric cost?

Assistant: (looking at the floor in embarrassment) That roll of material costs ten gold coins.

Customer: Good. I will take it. I really like it.

Narrator: And so the shop assistant was pleased with his work and he knew that the customer was delighted with her purchase. The next day the shopkeeper returned and instantly noticed that the roll of blue material was missing.

Shopkeeper: Did you sell the blue material?

Assistant: I did indeed, and not only that, I managed to get the proper price of ten gold coins for it. So that is good news, Sir.

Shopkeeper: No, it is not. It is terrible news. The material is faulty and we have been dishonest. I told you to sell it at half price. I must go and find the customer at once.

Assistant: But she was really pleased with it and thought the material was just right. You may never find her.

Shopkeeper: But I must find her.

Narrator: And so the shopkeeper went out into the crowded streets and kept asking people if they had seen a woman carrying a roll of blue material yesterday.

The shopkeeper approaches three members of the audience in different parts of the school hall asking if they saw a woman with a roll of blue material yesterday walking through the streets. On each occasion he gets the same negative answer.

Shopkeeper: Excuse me, but did you see a woman leave my shop yesterday carrying a roll of blue material?

Person in street: Yes I did, she lives in the large white house on the street to the left.

Shopkeeper: Thank you, I must go and see her.

Narrator: The shopkeeper made his way towards the house and knocked on the door. The woman came to the door.

Customer: Good morning, how can I help you?

Shopkeeper: Yesterday you visited my shop and my assistant sold you a roll of blue material but he charged the wrong price.

Customer: How dare you come round here and demand extra money! I paid a fair price yesterday.

Shopkeeper: You misunderstand. My assistant charged you too much. The material had a mark on it and it should have been half price. I have come to bring back half of your money.

Customer: Well, your honesty does you credit. As I said, I paid a fair price for it. I saw the mark straight away but knew I could work without using that part of the fabric. I am very happy with the purchase I made.

Shopkeeper: That may be true but I would always feel that I had cheated you and stolen your money. I insist you take five gold coins back.

33.

How Words Can Cause Damage

Three Star Assembly ⭐⭐⭐

Script

This image of a word cloud shows the key words used in today's story, and how often they are used. It clearly tells you that animals dominate the story, but it also shows you many of the positive words in the story as well as the negative ones. The story is a traditional Hindu tale about the importance of choosing your words carefully. It comes from the ancient scripts of the Panchatantra. This is a collection of Hindu fables, many of which are based around animals.

Story

Once upon a time in the long ago world, the birds realized they had no king and that this was not good enough. If they were to be successful they needed a leader who would guide them in the future. Long discussions took place between the birds to select their new king. Eventually it was agreed that they should be ruled by the wisest of all birds, and so they chose the owl. They set a day when the owl would be crowned and they announced that this would be a day of great celebration.

After a few weeks the great day of the coronation arrived and all the birds collected in a clearing in the woods to pay homage to their new leader. Just at the moment they were going to place a beautiful golden crown on his head, the crow flew overhead making a screeching sound. Suddenly the birds realized that the crow had not been at any of the meetings when the king was being chosen, and this was a very serious mistake.

'What shall we do? What shall we do?' they whispered urgently to each other. 'It is not right that the crow has not had his say or been allowed to vote.'

And so it was agreed that they would ask the crow straight away. They looked up and shouted, 'We have chosen the owl as our new king because he is the wisest of all birds. Do you agree that we have done the right thing?'

'I most certainly do not,' said the crow. 'Why him, and not a graceful swan, or a beautiful peacock, or a talkative parrot? Just look at the owl sat there on his padded cushion waiting to be crowned. He looks so evil and bad-tempered, and yet this is supposed to be the best day of his life. He is fierce and looks at everybody in such an unfriendly way. He is so ugly and there is no way we should have such an unpleasant looking king.'

The birds listened to the crow and started to say, 'We might have made a mess of this – the owl is a bit ugly and grumpy looking. Perhaps we'd better put off the coronation and think about it again on another day.' This was agreed and they flew off to their homes leaving the owl sat all alone on a deep red velvet cushion feeling rather sad. The only bird that was still around was the crow that had caused the problem in the first place.

The owl slowly turned to look at the crow and said, 'Why did you say all those terrible things? Why did you call me ugly and bad-tempered? I have always been kind and friendly to you. I have never harmed you in any way. I don't believe I will be ever able to speak to you again.' With that the owl soared away from the cushion and into the sky. This should have been the greatest day of his life and yet he was left feeling angry and sad.

And so now the crow was left all alone, and maybe for the first time he started to think about what he had said. It was true that the owl had never caused him any problems and had always been helpful. The crow felt sad that he had come along and wrecked his special day. He sat there on his own thinking, 'I have been so rude and terrible. My words have now caused so much damage. It is always wrong to say nasty things. In future I will only look for the best things in others and I will talk about them and celebrate them.' The crow called out to the owl, but by now he was now far away.

The crow was left alone cursing the mistakes he had made and wondering how he could put them right.

Questions to consider:

- What would be your message to the crow?

- What do you think the crow needs to learn to do better?

- As you look at the word cloud, see if you can identify the positive words and the effect they have on people and also the negative ones and their impact.

Please note that this assembly links well with the one on cyberbullying (see Chapter 43).

Four Star Assembly ★★★★

The assembly could start by going over some of the background to the Hindu religion:

- Hinduism is one of the world's oldest religions and has around one billion followers. There are around 500,000 Hindus in the UK. The majority have moved here over the last hundred years.

- Hindus believe in a supreme spirit – Brahman – which is present in all living things. Because of this there is a strong belief that it is wrong to harm any living thing.

- Hindus also believe in karma and that a person's actions and conduct in one life will determine what happens to them in the next life. If they live a life that is full of good actions then in the next life there will be a rebirth into a higher order.

Five Star Assembly ★★★★★

If time allows, you could work with a group of children to reflect on when their words have done damage to a friend, relative or classmate. This could be developed into a play script that could be performed in the assembly or a short story that could be read out. Alternatively, the children could be encouraged to write a poem describing their regret that could be used for quiet reflection.

34.
Wealth Does Not Make You a Rich Person

Three Star Assembly ✪✪✪

Script

This image shows a silver needle. It is so thin and so light. You could take it virtually anywhere and nobody would know you had it. Here is a very old story from the Sikh religion that involves such a needle. Let's see if you can find the meaning behind it.

Story

Guru Nanak frequently went travelling and he would preach and speak of his beliefs. He gathered many followers during this time, and this is a story from when he visited the great city of Lahore. Many of the people there were very poor. They didn't have proper homes and they were short of food. However, there were also many rich merchants who had built up great wealth. Duni Chand was the wealthiest of all and the richest man for miles around. He was so prosperous that he lived in a fabulous palace in which he had the finest jewels, the finest paintings and the finest ornaments. Duni Chand had a team of servants who looked after his every need. He lived in total luxury and he was very proud of everything he had achieved and all the money and wealth he had acquired.

Duni Chand also wanted everybody else to know how rich he was, and so he had flagpoles put up outside his palace. Each flag represented how rich he was. Every time he amassed a further 10,000 gold coins he added another flag, and soon there were seven flags.

When Duni Chand had heard that the famous Guru Nanak was visiting Lahore he knew that the local people would expect him to meet the Guru. It would be a marvellous opportunity to demonstrate to everybody just how important and how rich he was.

On the day that Guru Nanak was scheduled to visit Duni Chand's palace everything was looking perfect. An amazing feast had been planned and the best and most exotic foods were ordered. The finest musicians were going to perform and every room was decorated with the most beautiful fresh flowers. This was going to be the greatest banquet that Lahore had ever seen.

The evening proved to be a fabulous success and everyone agreed that everything had been perfect. As the evening was drawing to a close, Duni Chand looked up at Guru Nanak and said, 'I am a very rich man and you must have a gift so that you can remember your visit to my home. You can have absolutely anything you want – all you have to do is name it.'

There was a long period of silence and all the people could see that Guru Nanak was thinking very carefully. Eventually he reached into his pocket and pulled out a smart leather case containing the smallest of silver needles. Guru Nanak said, 'I don't need any gifts but I would like you to look after this very special needle for me and then when we meet again in the next life I

would like you to return it to me.' After handing over the precious silver needle, Guru Nanak thanked his host profusely for organizing such a splendid banquet and left.

Duni Chand could barely believe his luck. He thought he had been given a very important job. He was the person who had been trusted with looking after the special needle that belonged to Guru Nanak. He knew that everybody at the banquet was looking at him and thinking just how important he must be to have been selected to carry out this special task. However, the reality was very different because most of them had already worked out what had happened.

It was Duni Chand's wife who spoke next, saying, 'You idiot, you fool, you numbskull! Can't you see what has happened right under your nose? Don't you realize that everybody is laughing at you? You can't possibly take anything with you to the next life, it is impossible.'

All of a sudden Duni Chand felt extremely silly. He also realized that there was a reason he had been given the needle. He turned to his wife and urgently said, 'Guru Nanak is trying to give me a message. I must run after him and find out what it is.' So he set off running through the streets until he caught up with him. Gasping for breath he grabbed him by the shoulder and looked him in the eyes and said, 'Why did you give me this needle when you know that I can't take it with me to the next life?'

Guru Nanak looked up and said, 'But it's only a simple needle, and a very small one too. If you can't bring a thing as small as a needle with you, what are you going to do with all your gold coins, jewels and flags? Shouldn't you find a way of doing some good with all your money rather than simply showing off? If you can find good things to do with your money, then when you do pass through to the next life people will remember you not simply for being rich but for the rich deeds that you did.'

Duni Chand stopped and thought for a moment and when he looked up again Guru Nanak had disappeared through the streets. But those few words changed the lifestyle of Duni Chand, who went home to his wife and planned how he could help others.

Questions to consider:

■ What advice would you give Duni Chand?

■ Can you provide a title for this story in six powerful words?

Four Star Assembly ⭐⭐⭐⭐

If time allows, open the assembly by providing some background information about the Sikh religion and its importance in Britain today. The following notes may be helpful.

Sikhism is the fifth largest religion in the world with around 30 million followers. Sikhs believe there were ten great teachers and the first of these was Guru Nanak. He gave clear messages about how people should live their lives around the principles of humility, love, peace, truth and serving God. He said that these principles should be extended to people of all races and religions at all times, because all men and women are born equal and in order to love God you must learn to love one another. Followers of the Sikh religion also believe that they should work hard to make an honest living but also share their wealth with others. They also place great importance on the power of good deeds and will therefore often carry out voluntary work. Because Sikhs are so easily recognizable by their turbans they learn that they must always be seen to be doing good.

In a follow-up assembly children could research key elements of the Sikh faith, which could be turned into presentations. These could include:

• The Golden Temple in Amritsar.

• The Five Symbols of the Sikh religion.

• Sikh temples.

Five Star Assembly ★★★★★

You could extend the assembly further by particularly focusing on the Golden Temple in Amritsar. Its story captures the key elements of the Sikh faith.

Story

The Golden Temple in Amritsar was designed by Guru Ram Das who was a former leader of the religion. However, it was completed by his successor Guru Arjan. When it was being built many people thought it should be a very tall building that could be seen for miles around. However, Guru Arjan had other ideas and he said that the building should be low and that as people enter it they should have to go down several steps. This was because worshippers should feel humble and ready to serve God.

The temple was designed with four doors and this was also considered to be unusual. Guru Arjan explained that people from all directions should come to praise God and that they were to be welcomed to the temple regardless of where they originated. He believed the Temple was there for everyone. To demonstrate this point further, Guru Arjan invited a member of the Muslim faith to lay the foundation stone.

The purpose of this part of the book is to draw out the similarities between religions and advocate that there is more in the world that unites us than divides us. Therefore you could extend the assembly further by relating the clear messages in the story to similar ones in the New Testament. The best example is in Matthew 19:24, which is the story of a rich man who approaches Jesus and asks what he needs to do to be certain that he will be able to enter the kingdom of God. Jesus responds by stressing the importance of following each of the Ten Commandments. The man replies that he already does this. Jesus then commands the man to sell all his possessions and use the money for good deeds because it is harder for a rich person to enter the kingdom of God than for a camel to pass through the eye of a needle.

35.
A Story from the Buddha's Early Life

Three Star Assembly ★★★

Script

This image is a representation of the Buddha. Whilst Buddhism is a religion, it doesn't have a God and instead promotes the search for an inner, calm wisdom and deep understanding. Perhaps you can see that represented in the image. Two key words within the faith are *nirvana* and *karma*.

On Nirvana Day, which is celebrated by some Buddhists on 15 February, Buddhists think about their lives and how they can work towards gaining the perfect peace of nirvana. They remember friends or relations who have recently died and reflect on the fact that death is a part of life for everyone. The idea that nothing stays the same is central to Buddhism. Buddhists believe that loss and change are things to be accepted rather than causes of sadness. Through teachings about karma, Buddhists learn that our past actions affect us, either positively or negatively, and that our present actions will affect us in the future.

There are five key vows that a Buddhist makes, and one of them is not to hurt any living thing (the others are listed on page 179). Here is a story from the Buddha's early life, which includes this principle. The story also captures the true spirit of Buddhism.

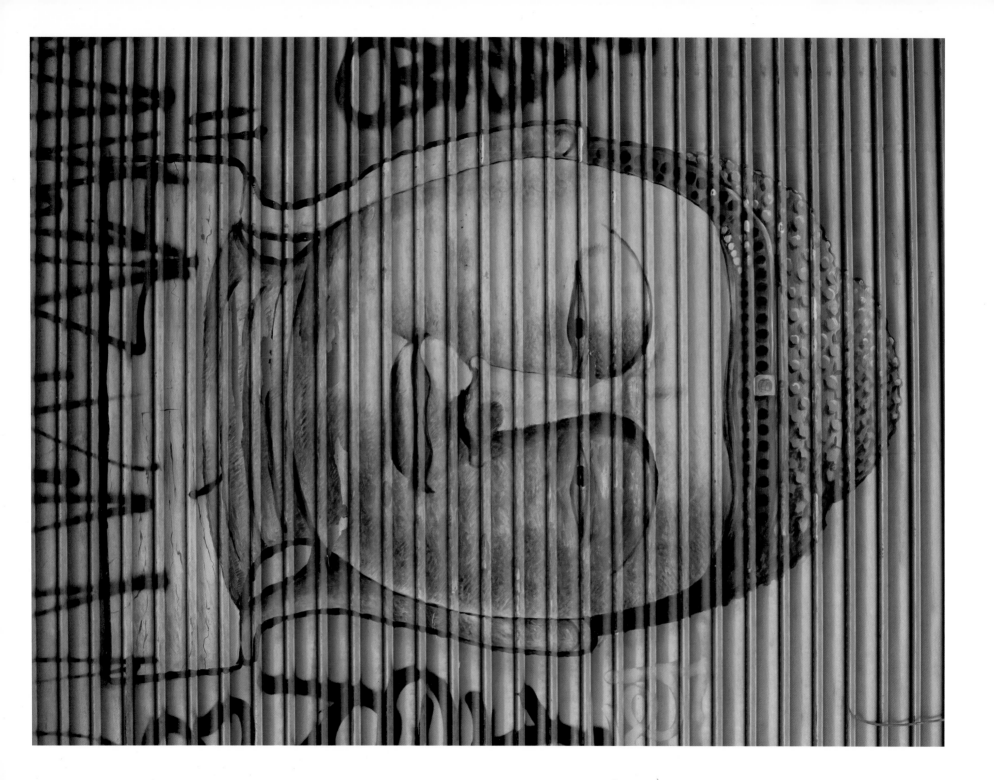

Story

One day, about 2,500 years ago, Prince Siddhartha was walking in his palace grounds and, as always, he was contemplating. He knew that in time he would become the king but he wasn't sure he wanted to be king. Instead he longed to travel and see many things. Some people from a very early age thought he was caring and had great wisdom. They thought he would make a great teacher.

The weather was fine and the sky was blue and eventually his eyes were drawn upwards towards the skies where a flock of swans were flying high overhead. The Prince was thinking how superb they looked as they soared by. He loved the speed and grace with which the mighty birds moved. But then an arrow sped through the skies, striking the lead swan and bringing it crashing to the ground.

The Prince raced over to the swan to see if it was still alive. He was desperately hoping he would be able to save it. The swan was still breathing but it was rapidly losing blood. Prince Siddhartha knew that if he was going to stand any chance of saving the bird's life he had to remove the arrow and ease the animal's pain. The swan was clearly frightened but seemed to have trust in the young boy who was now cradling it and speaking in a soft and gentle way. Finally, he wrapped his shirt around the swan and began moving it inside and away from the heat of the sun.

Just then Prince Siddhartha heard excited shrieks coming towards him. 'I shot it, I shot it and it came crashing to the ground. I shot the lead swan!' It was the voice of one of his cousins who was clearly feeling very pleased with himself. When he saw the Prince holding the swan his cousin started shouting once more, 'Hey that's my swan, I shot it – give it to me.'

But there was no way that Prince Siddhartha was going to give up the swan because he knew it would be killed. A heated argument developed with the Prince's cousin claiming the swan was his because he had shot it and the Prince claiming it was his because he was looking after it. It was clear that neither of them was going to give in. Both of the boys were convinced that they were absolutely right and the swan rightfully belonged to them. I wonder which of the boys you believe the swan belonged to?

Finally they agreed that they would return to the palace and go to the courtroom and ask one of the judges to rule on who should keep the swan. The Prince's cousin explained how he shot the bird and why it should be his, while Prince Siddhartha explained how he found the bird and why it was therefore his.

The judge thought long and hard because both boys seemed to be right in what they said. By now quite a crowd had gathered to see what would happen next. Eventually the judge reached his decision and slowly began to speak: 'The most valuable thing we have is life. It is the most precious gift we are given. One boy did not value the life of this beautiful swan and tried to remove its life. The other boy did value the life of the swan and tried to save it. I therefore rule that Prince Siddhartha should have the swan. Now we should let him leave and see if he can nurse the bird back to life and then, if he is successful, he should set it free once more.'

■ Take another look at the image of the Buddha – what qualities do you see in the person?

■ Do you understand the concepts of nirvana and karma, and how Buddhists live their lives to achieve perfect peace?

■ Can you provide a title for this story using six powerful words?

Four Star Assembly ✪ ✪ ✪ ✪

You could introduce the assembly by providing background information about Buddhism.

Story

Some people consider Buddhism to be a religion without a god. The Buddha was believed to have lived over 2,500 years ago as Prince Siddhartha. Throughout his childhood he spent much time trying to make reason out of the world. He tried to learn from each experience he had – and today's story is one example.

Prince Siddhartha never did become a king. He left the palace to lead a very simple life and claimed he wanted to become awakened to the real life around him. As he learned more and more he started to teach and the people called him the 'Buddha' or the 'enlightened one'.

There are more than a billion Buddhists in the world today and in Britain approximately 150,000 people claim to be Buddhists.

The Buddha taught his followers to lead a life of meditation, morality and wisdom. He taught that there four noble truths:

1. That all life contains suffering.

2. That suffering is caused by selfishness.

3. That suffering will be avoided by overcoming selfishness.

4. That suffering will end if we follow the eight-point path of:

   ◆ Understanding

   ◆ Thinking clearly

   ◆ Saying the right things

- Doing the right things
- Doing a valuable job
- Recognizing the importance of hard work
- Being mindful and alert
- Contemplation

Buddhists make five vows, which guide them in all their actions:

1. Not to harm any living thing.
2. Not to take what is not given.
3. Not to misuse your senses.
4. Not to speak wrongly.
5. Not to use drugs or alcohol.

Five Star Assembly ⭐⭐⭐⭐⭐

There are many simple Buddhist prayers that could be used for quiet reflection to conclude the assembly. Here are two that clearly reflect the Buddhist way of life – the words have been slightly adapted:

May all living beings have happiness and the causes of happiness;

May all living beings be free from misery and the causes of misery;

May all living beings never be separated from happiness, and be devoid of misery;

May all living beings abide in equality and free from prejudice.

I will do all the good I can

In all the ways I can

In all the places I can

For as long as I can.

36.

But I Thought My Son Was Dead: The Story of a Modern-Day Prodigal Son

Three Star Assembly ✦✦✦

Script

Take a look at the image: nearly everybody is in a hurry. Maybe they are rushing to work or to the shops, or even home. One person remains static – he has no job or home to go to and no money to spend. He is desperate. The Parable of the Prodigal Son in the Bible tells of such a person. Today we will give the story a twenty-first century focus.

Story

Three of the finest electrical shops in the county – that was William Henderson's claim to fame. It was now over thirty years since he had opened his first outlet in a rundown unit in a small back street and through hard work and always keeping up to date with the latest technology, the business was as strong as ever. Other bigger shops were closing down but not Henderson's.

William was looking around one of his shops. It was filled with plasma TVs, laptops, MP3 players and every modern-day gadget imaginable. In the corner, one of his sons was leading a lesson on how to use some of the software on a new tablet computer.

Despite his success, all was not well for William Henderson. He was deeply troubled. He had two sons, James and Sam. Both were now young men in their early twenties. They had joined the business and were doing well. William and his sons each managed one of the three shops and business was booming. However, the night before Sam had told his father he wanted to leave.

James had seen the trouble coming one day when he was in the warehouse with Sam. The two boys normally had a lot of laughs – the warehouse was where they unwound and relaxed – but not on this particular day. Sam had looked up and said, 'Have you ever thought what all this is worth? There must be thousands of pounds worth of equipment just sitting here waiting to be sold. Why don't we just pack it all in and go and see the world?'

But James enjoyed working for the business and he was loyal to his father. He had no plans to leave. Later that night Sam asked his father, 'When you die I will get a share of all the money the shops have made. But I am a young man full of energy and I want to travel the world and enjoy life rather than working in a shop every day. Can I have my share of the money now?'

William had spent all night thinking about Sam's request and he knew he would have to say yes. He loved his son deeply and would really miss him, but he didn't want to make him stay against his will.

Within a few weeks William had made the financial arrangements and Sam was gone. James was extremely angry about Sam being handed such a huge amount of money and then suddenly finding he was now having to do twice as much work. By the time Sam drove off he was glad to see the back of his brother; at least he wouldn't have to talk to him again.

Sam made his way from city to city. He was having a great time. To start with he sent text messages and emails home but these soon started to dry up. He regularly bought rounds of drinks for his many new-found friends when they visited bars and casinos. Sam was enjoying life and having a lot of fun, but he was also drinking heavily and then his friends encouraged him to try drugs.

The problem was that Sam was now spending so fast that the money was running out. It seemed like he spent more and more each day. Soon it would run out and he would have nowhere to stay and no money to buy food. He went to his friends to ask if he could move in with them or if they would buy the food tonight, but all of a sudden they were nowhere to be seen. They had been happy while Sam was paying out for them but they weren't prepared to help Sam now that he was in need.

There followed six months of misery for Sam. He sold his car. His clothes were growing old and tatty. He had tried to get a job but times were hard and very few people were taking on staff, and besides, he was looking so scruffy that people didn't want to employ him.

It was on the 4th of November that Sam was evicted from the house where he was staying. By then he hadn't paid any rent for two months. He walked alone through the streets. It was cold and there was drizzle in the air. He walked past a man who said, 'Big Issue, Sir?' and added, 'Have a nice day' as Sam made his way silently past.

Have a nice day, thought Sam to himself. When did I last have a really nice day? It certainly hadn't been for several months. He knew that while he had money people had used him and that all he had been doing really was showing off. And now he was paying the price for his stupidity. He was alone and homeless. In fact, the last time he had been truly happy was when he had been working in the shop with his father and brother. For the next few hours he couldn't get that thought out of his mind. As he walked through the streets it was as though a voice kept saying, 'Go home, go home'. At least his father and James might give him a job, any job, even if it was simply sweeping the floors of the warehouse.

And so Sam hitched rides and hid on the back of trucks until eventually he arrived at the drive to his father's house. He was tired, dirty and unshaven. He looked at the two cars parked outside the house. He remembered when his car would have been there too, and then fear took over. He wanted to knock on the door but he daren't. He had gone off with his father's money and made a complete mess of his life. The tears ran down his cheeks as he thought about the damage he had done. He turned to move off down the street thinking he could never return.

As he moved away the door to the house was flung open. A voice shouted, 'Sam, Sam, come back!' Sam turned to see his father running towards him with his arms wide open. Sam froze until he felt his father's arms wrap around him. His father spoke next saying, 'Every day I have watched that driveway hoping that one day you would walk back up it. You may not look like the smart young man who left, but as soon as you stood there I knew it was you. Please come inside, you look like you need a warm bath, decent clothes and a good meal.'

Sam and his father made their way into the house but James wasn't happy to see his brother. He was about to leave in a storm of anger, yelling: 'This isn't fair. He has gone away and wasted all his money having a good time while I have stayed here working, and now you're making such a huge fuss saying how glad you are that he has returned! I have been here every day working hard for the business and never once have you said how glad you are that I am here!'

His father looked at him and said, 'James, you have truly been a good son to me. You have been here every day and you have been loyal to me. I should have said thank you to you more often, and one day you will get your full share of the money. However, these last months have been very difficult for me. Every day that Sam has been away I have worried about him and when the texts and emails stopped coming I even thought he could be dead. But look, your brother is here. He is alive and well and has come home. Please come and celebrate with us.'

For a long time there was a deep tension between the two boys. James thought that Sam would disappear again as soon as he had some money, but he didn't. And the strange thing is that now they can be often seen laughing and joking together in the warehouse.

Questions to consider:

- Take a look at the image and consider which powerful words you would use to describe the lonely, homeless man.

- Can you try to describe what the man might feel like using just six words?

- What sorts of bad things could happen such that a person could end up becoming homeless?

- In the story James wanted his father to turn his back on Sam, but he didn't because he wanted to give him a second chance. Are there ways in which we can help vulnerable people to have a second chance?

Four Star Assembly ✪✪✪✪

Script

The assembly could also be used to revise some of the key principles of Christianity.

Most of you will recognize that this story is an adaptation of the Prodigal Son, which can be found in the New Testament (Luke 15:11–32).

Followers of the Christian faith believe in one God who created all things and is always present. Another central belief is that Jesus is the Son of God and that he died to save the human race. Christians also believe he rose from the dead. The conviction that Jesus was both God and human is significant in the Christian faith.

The teachings of Jesus are a guide to help Christians live a good life. Much of his teaching comes in the form of stories which can be found in the New Testament. These stories have stood the test of time and are as meaningful today as they were 2,000 years ago.

Five Star Assembly ✪✪✪✪✪

To complete the assembly you could read out the original story from Luke or ask one of the learners to do so. While it is being read the children could reflect silently on the story.

37.
Let Nobody Steal Your Dreams (Especially Teachers!)

Three Star Assembly ⭐ ⭐ ⭐

This is an assembly that is only suitable for a teacher or school leader who accepts that sometimes teachers get it wrong!

Script

This image shows a group of children who have the capacity to do great things in their lives. Each will have a dream of what they might do in the future. Sometimes teachers and adults help children to achieve their dreams but sometimes they don't. All of us are born with wonderful talents. Schools should help their students to discover these talents and become successful individuals. This is an assembly about people with great determination and personality who proved their teachers wrong.

Story

A boy called Richard Reed found himself in serious trouble at school because he had been selling Smurf stickers to the other children in his class. He was told it was wrong to make money by selling things at a profit and that he must never do it again. Many years later, he started to make fruit drinks and sold them at a music festival. Those people who bought the drinks really enjoyed them and said he should make more, and so he did. After that he made even more and set up a company called Innocent. Today he sells lots of smoothies and fruit juices and makes lots of money. I wonder if his teacher wishes he had given Richard a bit more encouragement rather than telling him off.

When he was about to leave school, Matt Groening was told to stop writing silly stories and drawing cartoons because he would never make money from them. He was advised that he should look for a more sensible career and become a doctor or a lawyer or a teacher. But instead, he just carried on with his stories and pictures. Perhaps he should have listened to his teachers, but if he had then one of the most popular television shows ever wouldn't have been created – *The Simpsons* – and he wouldn't have won so many awards or made so much money! When he was young, one of Matt Groening's teachers was called Elizabeth Hoover. She recognized Matt's talents and told him that she loved his stories and pictures. Today she is a character in the show. Every episode of *The Simpsons* has been watched by millions of viewers all over the world. Each show has been shown time and time again but still people watch. It has made Matt Groening a very successful and rich man, but I wonder if his unsupportive teachers now feel rather silly.

Two famous musicians called John Lennon and Paul McCartney didn't do very well at school. On John's school report it said that he was 'hopeless' and 'a clown in class' and that he was 'on the road to nowhere'. Paul claims that he spent much of his days in school getting into trouble because he was daydreaming about the future rather than concentrating on his lessons, which he thought were boring. However, when they were close to leaving school the two boys had a very strange experience.

On the same night, John and Paul had exactly the same dream. In it they had gone out into the garden and started to dig with their bare hands. It was hard and gruelling work because they had no tools and in their dream they were soon covered in dirt and sweat was dripping from them. Their hands became sore and started to bleed, but still they carried on digging. Eventually they found a gold coin buried deep in the soil, and then another gold coin, and

then more and more coins were found. The next day they talked about the dream they had shared and tried to work out what it meant. Eventually they came to the conclusion that it meant if they dug deep into their resolve, worked really hard and used their talents well, then gold and wealth would come their way.

And they did work hard and several decades later The Beatles continue to sell millions of records. During their career they performed in front of huge audiences and their music is still played on radio stations around the world. I wonder if their teachers still think they were hopeless and on the road to nowhere.

All teachers should consider this thought: every individual has great talents. Some of these abilities will quickly come to the surface while others may be brought out by other people, such as teachers. Will you be opening the door and looking for those talents or banging the door closed on them?

Questions to consider:

- Have you got a dream of how you will use your talents and through hard work make a difference to the world? If you have, think about it, work hard and don't let anybody steal it.

- Now take a look at the image again and consider whether young people all over the world receive the same opportunities. Are there things that your school might be able to do to support other, less advantaged, children?

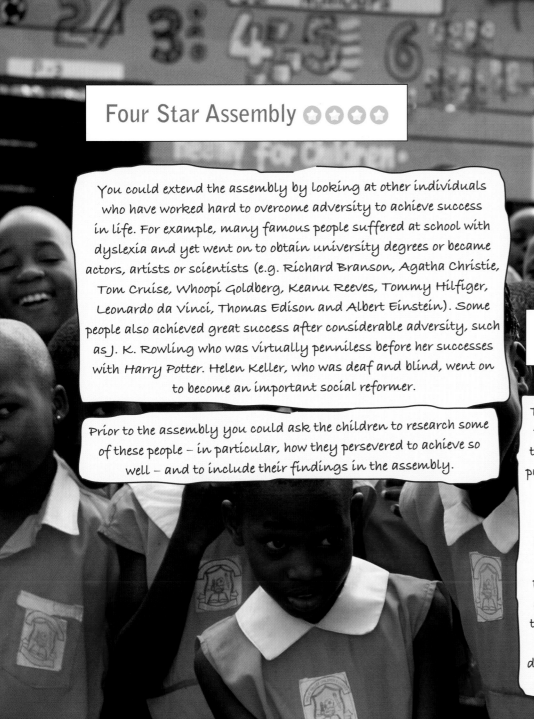

Four Star Assembly ⭐⭐⭐⭐

You could extend the assembly by looking at other individuals who have worked hard to overcome adversity to achieve success in life. For example, many famous people suffered at school with dyslexia and yet went on to obtain university degrees or became actors, artists or scientists (e.g. Richard Branson, Agatha Christie, Tom Cruise, Whoopi Goldberg, Keanu Reeves, Tommy Hilfiger, Leonardo da Vinci, Thomas Edison and Albert Einstein). Some people also achieved great success after considerable adversity, such as J. K. Rowling who was virtually penniless before her successes with *Harry Potter*. Helen Keller, who was deaf and blind, went on to become an important social reformer.

Prior to the assembly you could ask the children to research some of these people – in particular, how they persevered to achieve so well – and to include their findings in the assembly.

Five Star Assembly ⭐⭐⭐⭐⭐

This assembly is as much for the teachers sat around the edge of the hall as for the children. It is important that teachers are able to recognize the talents of all pupils and not discourage them by putting labels on them. So are you brave enough for the next step?

If so, come up with a list of famous people who didn't perform well in school, who left with no qualifications or who truanted (e.g. Simon Cowell, Alan Sugar, Christine Aguilera, Billy Joel, Martin Luther King, Judy Dench, Jacqueline Wilson and J. K. Rowling). Ask a group of children in each class to produce their own list. Then ask the teacher and the children to consider what these young people may have needed less of in the classroom and what they needed more of, so that their talents may have been discovered sooner. Alternatively, the school council could consider this question and their views fed back into the assembly.

38.
The Circle of Life: Where Will I Go?

Three Star Assembly ✪✪✪

Script

Take a look at the image of a man gazing into the sun and contemplating the beauty of the earth. Today, we will open the assembly by listening to the opening words of the song 'Circle of Life' from *The Lion King.*

Show the lyrics from the first verse. These can be found on the Internet: http://www.lionking.org/lyrics/OMPS/CircleOfLife.html>

The 'Circle of Life' tells of the fabulous world we live in and the range of places there are to visit. It tells of the potential things we can learn and also suggests we have much to do if we are to leave the world a better place.

The start of the year (or school year) is a good time to reflect on what we will achieve in life. Ask the children to give ambitious answers to the following questions because it is good to have big goals in life.

Questions to consider:

◼ Which places in the world would you like to stand and gaze at?

◼ What would you really like to know lots about?

◼ What would you like to do to make the world a better place?

◼ What would you like to achieve in the next year?

◼ What do you need to do to bring your dreams to reality?

In order to stimulate the children's thinking, the person leading the assembly could provide their own responses to some of the questions.

Four Star Assembly ✪✪✪✪

The assembly can be extended in a variety of ways. The use of the music or video footage from *The Lion King* is an obvious example. Film footage displaying the lyrics is available on the internet. If the person leading the assembly is up for a challenge, they could identify a new skill they would like to learn over the year, such as playing a musical instrument or learning to dance. The teacher could then demonstrate how good (or poor!) they are at this skill at present and promise to reveal how they have improved by the end of the year. If revisited regularly during the year, this can be a very effective way both to demonstrate the trials and tribulations related to new learning and to emphasize the importance of resilience and perseverance.

Five Star Assembly ✪✪✪✪✪

The 'Circle of Life' song suggests there is much we can do in the world, so set the children a challenge on how they could help to improve the world over the next year through their work within enterprise education. For example, each year group could adopt a charity and research its work over the course of a year. Classes could then lead assemblies about their chosen charities to help develop the awareness of the other children. This is done best through each year group selecting a different type of charity (e.g. conservation/wildlife charity, children's charity, charity that supports older people, provides overseas aid, supports war victims or relates to a serious illness).

Themes: Stereotyping, good and bad uses of technology
Parable of the Good Samaritan
Timing: General

39.
The Parable of the Good Hoodies

Three Star Assembly ✪✪✪

Script

Take a look at the image of a group of boys hanging around on a street corner. How would you feel if you had to walk past them? I wonder what words you might use to describe the gang or your own feelings about them. Today, we have a tale of the unexpected which places a Bible story in a twenty-first century context.

Story

Dear old Mrs Petridis never looked forward to her journey home in the dark. She had been to see her sister in hospital. She especially didn't like walking past the supermarket on the corner because there was always a gang of youths hanging about wearing hoodies. They seemed sinister standing around drinking from cans and bottles. Sometimes they shouted at their older friends who drove past in souped-up cars. On other occasions, a lad would park his car outside, lift the bonnet and simply rev the engine while the gang huddled over listening to its throaty roar. Mrs Petridis's walk home had seemed even more frightening since she'd seen some footage of riots on the television. Even after she got past the supermarket, there was still the problem of the subway and that was really scary. The lighting was often broken, litter was scattered across the floor and it often seemed to be a shelter to even more groups of teenage boys.

She held her shopping bag tightly as she passed the shop. As always, the gang stood there with their hoods up. As always, they looked menacing and she expected them to start shouting at her but they didn't. She felt their eyes drilling into her. She tried to move away as quickly as she could, but at the age of 78 that was never going to be fast enough for her to feel comfortable. Eventually, after what seemed an age, the gang were a hundred metres behind her and she was at the top of the twenty-five steps down into the subway. She always counted the steps down and the steps up. It was like measuring her route to safety. The traffic raced by on the main road overhead.

Mrs Petridis started the journey down the steps, 'One, two, three, four.' Well, at least it seemed quiet in the subway today. 'Thirteen, fourteen, fifteen.' Then she started to think about the warm soup she would eat when she got home. 'Twenty-one, twenty-two, twenty-three …' *Crash!* All of a sudden Mrs Petridis missed her footing and fell in a heap at the bottom, her bags tumbling out of her hand. She quickly came to her senses and thought, well, thank heavens nobody saw me – I feel so silly. She moved to put her weight on her ankle to stand up and a piercing pain shot up her leg. All of a sudden she realized she was trapped on the floor and in total agony. And then she felt the warm drop of blood trickling down her forehead. Her home and warm soup felt a very long way away, and she knew that the gang of youths was not far behind her.

At that moment she heard footsteps coming from one of the other entrances to the subway. She looked up and saw a smartly dressed man with a briefcase about 15 metres away. She called out to him for help. He looked at her then mumbled something about drunks and sped up and rushed away. She tried to move but the pain was too much. She said to herself, oh dear, whatever shall I do next? Then she saw a young woman carrying a laptop. She was talking to someone on her mobile phone and laughing. Once again, Mrs Petridis called out but the woman carried on with her conversation and walked on. The last thing she heard her say down the phone was 'What noise? Oh, it's just some old woman lying on the floor.'

Just when things couldn't get any worse, suddenly they did. The gang of hoodies had left the entrance to the supermarket and were heading down the steps into the subway singing football songs. She curled herself into a ball wondering what they would do to her. Would they laugh and point or kick her or steal her bags? Not only that, she feared they would take photographs with their mobile phones and put them on the Internet so that everyone could laugh at her. Mrs Petridis hated mobile phones. She thought they were bad things and caused a lot of trouble. She clutched her handbag to protect her purse and braced herself for the worst.

The singing and shouting suddenly stopped. Then she heard one of them shout, 'Look, it's the old woman who walks past the shop – she's fallen. Quick, help her to her feet.'

Omar spoke next, 'No, remember that first aid training at school – we could do more damage. Talk to her first and see if she's in pain.'

Two of the gang bent over Mrs Petridis and asked how she was. One of them took out tissues to mop up the blood on her head. The other spoke softly to her to find out what had happened. Shocked by the response, Mrs Petridis told them about the pain in her ankle and leg, but she still gripped her handbag very tightly because she feared it would be stolen by one of the gang. Omar took control at this point and said, 'Shane, give me your hoodie to put under her head to make her comfortable. Smithy, your house is two minutes away and your mum is a nurse – get on your mobile and get her here. She will make sure we're doing the right things. Danno, use your mobile to get an ambulance.'

Twenty-four hours later, Mrs Petridis was sat at home watching television. She had her feet up on a stool – one leg was in plaster. She kept thinking about the bunch of hoodies who had rescued her; the same gang that she had feared. The only thing that had gone wrong was that she'd somehow lost one of her shopping bags but that really didn't matter.

A short while later the boys came calling at her house, but this time their hoodies were gone. They looked very different in their school uniforms and carrying bags with their carefully completed course work. They announced that they had come to see how she was. They told her that they always called her 'the nice old lady in the brown coat' and added that they had come to return her shopping bag. Danno spoke next: 'Your shopping bag has got some soup in it – shall I heat it up for you? Oh, and another thing, you ought to carry a mobile phone. They are really good things – they could save your life when you're in trouble.'

Questions to consider:

- What message do you think this story has for Mrs Petridis?

- What message would you want to give to the passers-by who ignored her?

- Can you provide a title for the story using six, powerful words?

Four Star Assembly ⭐⭐⭐⭐

This assembly could be extended in a variety of ways involving the children. However, preparation and rehearsal would be needed. A good idea would be to focus on the man with the briefcase who thought Mrs Petridis was drunk and the young woman with the mobile phone. Imagine they have arrived home and they are talking to their wife or husband and suddenly the scene in the subway comes back to them. Maybe they even saw the ambulance heading towards the incident. They now realize they might have made a serious error. Get the children to plan the conversation that could have taken place with their partners, but aim to get them to end it with an action that the man or woman will take if they witness a similar situation in the future.

An alternative activity would to ask the children to think of good uses and bad uses of mobile phones.

Five Star Assembly ⭐⭐⭐⭐⭐

This story is based on the Parable of the Good Samaritan (Luke 10:25-37). You could consider reading the parable to the children while the children reflect quietly. Alternatively, the children could perform the story or make a Flip Video of a group performing it. There are also numerous children's versions of the parable readily available on the Internet.

40.

Can Starfish Children Make a Difference?

Three Star Assembly ⭐ ⭐ ⭐

The shape of things to come...

Script

Take a look at the image and dwell on the caption on the decaying building. How you would describe the scene. It looks a little desolate with the barbed wire coiled around the building. The purpose of today's assembly is to explore which parts of our community are beautiful and give us pleasure, and which parts are unsightly and we would prefer to avoid. So just spend a minute thinking quietly about the school grounds, the roads and streets, the parks and fields around our school. In your mind you could imagine walking from home to school – you could even visualize doing it in the different seasons of the year. Try to use as many senses as possible and consider what you can see, hear, touch and smell.

Then think of as many things of beauty that you really like. Some of these could be natural and others may be manmade. These might include trees coming into bud, birdsong, bulbs flowering in the springtime or a fun playground. Next think of as many things that are ugly and spoil the community. These might include litter, graffiti, the noise of traffic or boarded up buildings.

Use a flip chart to collect the children's examples and list them under the appropriate column: beautiful or ugly. Try to write at least ten entries in each column. Then focus on the ugly column and identify those things that the children might be able to do something about or even make a positive difference and turn it into something beautiful. Extend the list in this column with any suitable examples.

When you have done this, tell the children the starfish story.

Story

One upon a time, a boy was walking along the beach with his father. It was nearly dusk and the light was failing. It would soon be dark. The tide was going out leaving the sand shiny and wet. Many starfish had been washed up onto the beach from the stormy seas earlier in the day. The boy was having great fun picking them up and placing them back in the sea.

However, his father was growing impatient. He desperately wanted to get home before the light failed. He was looking forward to a warm drink and relaxing in front of the fire, watching the football on television. He looked at his son and said, 'Come along now, we need to get home.' But the young boy didn't seem to be listening. He simply carried on returning starfish to the sea.

His father spoke again, this time with more determination, 'Come on, son. Your mum is waiting. We need to get home.' But still the boy carried starfish back to the water as though he hadn't heard.

The boy's father was now growing angry and snapped, 'Leave the starfish, we need to get home. You aren't listening to me.'

The little boy looked up, and said, 'I was listening, but the starfish belong in the sea and so I'm putting them back.'

The boy's father dropped his voice this time and softly said, 'But just look around you. There are hundreds of them – you will never make a difference!'

The little boy bent down one final time, picked up a starfish and said, 'Well, I made a difference to that one.'

Questions to consider:

- Take another look at the image and think of as many powerful words as possible that describe the scene. Could you illustrate it in a powerful six-word story?

- Think about the list we made earlier about unsightly things in the neighbourhood – which of these can we make a difference to and how could this be achieved?

Four Star Assembly ✪✪✪✪

There are various ways in which the assembly could be extended. Songs such as The Pogues' 'Dirty Old Town' or Louis Armstrong's 'What a Wonderful World' could be used as an introduction.

You could also work with children to complete a sensory trail around the local area. Take a class of children out into the neighbourhood and ask them to use all their senses to pick out the things they really like about their locality and those things that displease them. Ask the children to focus on powerful adjectives that capture their feelings. An interesting way of presenting their work is to create a poem in which they systematically use each letter of the alphabet in turn to begin each line.

When outdoors, ask the children to draw some observational sketches to support their sensory trail and include both the writing and the sketches in the assembly.

Another option would be to get the children to create a pollution map of the local area.

Five Star Assembly ✪✪✪✪✪

The children could build on their sensory trail and carry out some more analytical investigations. For example, they could evaluate the type of litter found in a particular square metre of ground, make recordings to analyse noise pollution where there is heavy traffic or use double-sided sticky tape to collect evidence of dust particle pollution. The children could use this research to write letters to local government asking them to pursue change.

However, the ultimate challenge will come if they take responsibility for improving their community. For example, they could clean up a particular area or run mini-businesses to raise funds to transform a problem area into a place of beauty. If they can do this, they will be like the little boy in the starfish story and make a real difference.

201

41.
A Real Friend Walks In When the Rest of the World Walks Out

Three Star Assembly ★ ★ ★

Script

Take a look at this image. It shows two children who look as if they are totally happy in each other's company. They seem like they have a very special friendship, but I wonder what makes a really powerful friendship.

Story

Daniel always arrived at school early and he was always the last to go home. The longer he was there for, he thought, the more likely it would be that he might make a friend, but throughout all his school years he had never achieved success on a lasting basis.

Maybe the other children were repelled by his appearance. Daniel never looked as smart as everyone else. Their bright red sweatshirts were always clean and freshly washed. Daniel's clothes were often grubby and stained with bits of spilled food. Instead of designer trainers Daniel wore a pair of battered old lace-up shoes.

Or perhaps the other children were put off by the fact that Daniel often got himself into trouble. He found classroom work difficult. His exercise books often had lots of mistakes in them and the crossings out made his work look very messy. Sometimes when he really got stuck he would shout at his teacher and throw things on the floor. This frightened the other pupils. When it came to group work, nobody wanted to be with Daniel. Everybody knew he lost his temper very quickly. Daniel had regular meetings with the learning mentor but so far there had been little improvement.

Whenever a new child arrived at school, Daniel would be quick to try to build a friendship with them. He would run up and offer to look after them and show them around the school. All of which was a good thing to do, but sometimes he would then do the wrong thing. He often stole things from other children and gave them to the new student as a gift. It was as though he was trying to buy friends.

One day a new boy arrived in school called Marek. He came from Poland and spoke very little English. He seemed very frightened by his new surroundings and the other children in the class did little to help. They didn't want to play with him because he seemed very different. He couldn't speak to anyone and so he didn't, and they didn't speak to him. Each night he lay in his bed crying himself to sleep because he felt so lonely and he desperately wanted to go home to Poland. On this occasion even Daniel didn't try to make friends with Marek because he thought it would make the other children in the class hate him even more.

There were an increasing number of Eastern European families in the area. In fact, a Polish family now owned the local corner shop that the children visited after school. They had made a lot of improvements to the store but many of the children had stopped going. The locals said, 'It's different now somehow.'

It was a Tuesday lunchtime when the accident happened. Not a major disaster but in some ways a life changing accident. Daniel had just collected his school dinner and was carefully carrying his tray towards his seat when … *crash*. He slipped on some spilled custard and suddenly he was flat on the floor. His dinner flew in the air and splattered all over his face. He was hurting from his fall and he was expecting the other children to laugh and point at him because he had made a fool of himself. He hated it when people laughed at him. His face turned bright red and he felt as though his brain would explode. Whoever was the nearest person would certainly know about it because Daniel would likely push them to the floor to see how they liked it.

However, as he looked up no one was laughing or pointing. Marek was standing there. Daniel was about to get up and push him over, but Marek was holding out his hand to pull him up. He said in the little bit of English he knew, 'I help'.

The anger drained away from Daniel and instead of pushing Marek over he reached out to take the helping hand. That split-second decision helped to transform both boys. The only other person who noticed what had happened was the learning mentor. She had watched and thought, I wonder … Over the next few days and weeks she created opportunities for them to work and play together and a bond started to develop. Marek learned English from the two of them. They played board games to learn turn-taking and sometimes, when things had gone well, they had a treat and walked up to the shop. The friendship grew and blossomed and, as it did so, Daniel found he got into less trouble at school and this meant he became more popular with the other children. Now sometimes a whole crowd of them will go to the sweetshop.

Questions to consider:

- Take another look at the image – why do you think the two boys might have a special friendship, and what kind of things do you think they do together?

- What activities do you do with your friends? When might you need to stick together?

- Having a friend makes it easier to feel positive about life and this can help you to become successful in what you do. What qualities would a true friend have and how might they influence you?

Another idea would be to read the story to a class or group of children prior to the assembly as part of a Philosophy for Children exercise. The children could then reflect on the key questions that emerge from the story and then focus on one in a community of enquiry. The children could also reflect on some of the side issues in the story, such as stereotyping children by their appearance, or the feelings and fears of children who are new arrivals to a country or location or issues of racism that could occur when the population of a community starts to change.

In addition, you could ask the children to consider what message they would give to:

- Daniel

- Marek

- The other children in the class

- The learning mentor

The outcomes of this work can be fed into the final assembly.

Four Star Assembly ✪ ✪ ✪ ✪

You could consider closing the assembly with a famous poem about friendship such as 'The Arrow and the Song' by Henry Wadsworth Longfellow, 'A Time to Talk' by Robert Frost or 'I Knew a Man by Sight' by David Henry Thoreau. There are numerous websites that could help you find more recent examples. The poems could also be used for quiet reflection.

Five Star Assembly ✪ ✪ ✪ ✪ ✪

There is a brilliant short film by Neil Coslett called *Killing Time at Home* which could be used to introduce the assembly. It is available on the Internet and it could help to open up a debate around what is disposable in our lives and the importance of friendship. It could also be useful for a Philosophy for Children activity.

42.
Caring in a Community

Three Star Assembly ✪✪✪

Script

This image shows a homeless person sleeping rough on the streets in the middle of winter. This is a scene repeated all over the world. Most people walk past without a second thought but during today's assembly we are going to consider how we show kindness and caring, but first of all here comes a true story from India.

Story

This is the famous story of Bhagat Puran Singh who was born in India as Ramji Das. He later became a Sikh and was therefore highly committed to working hard and doing good deeds that would benefit his community. His family had been bankers and this meant that he'd had a relatively wealthy upbringing, but when the family business collapsed Puran Singh was forced to look for work elsewhere. Eventually he travelled to the city of Lahore where he hoped to find a job.

However, as he looked around the city he found many things that worried him. There was great poverty and also much illness and disease. This concerned Puran Singh and made him think deeply about what was happening. He thought to himself: 'In the streets, there are old people and newborn babies no one wants to look after. There are disabled and ill people who are not admitted into any of the hospitals and are left to die on the roadside. There are diseased persons no one wants to touch, but who is there to look after all of these people?'[1] The only answer Puran Singh could come up with was nobody.

One day as he was walking around the city, he came across a severely disabled boy who could not speak and had great difficulty in moving. The boy had no money and nobody to look after him. At that moment Puran Singh realized how lucky he was to be healthy and that, instead of finding a job and making money for himself, he would dedicate his energies towards supporting the poor, the ill and the lonely. He wanted these people to feel kindness and love. The only problem was that he had no money and most medical treatment was very expensive.

Puran Singh worked hard to raise funds in Lahore and eventually he travelled to the Golden Temple in Amritsar, which receives thousands of visitors every year. He encouraged the people visiting the Temple to donate money so he could continue his work. With the funds he raised, he set up a small campsite of tents and soon they were filled with people desperately needing a home, safety or medical treatment. When people were ill he took them to the hospital, sometimes carrying them there himself.

People from miles around started to notice the work of Puran Singh and their admiration for him grew. They listened carefully to what he had to say. He told them that the nation should not be judged on the wealth within its treasury but on the character of its people. Before long they started to bring gifts of money,

blankets and clothing. The doctors and nurses did their bit too and often worked free of charge.

As the story of Bhagat Puran Singh's work spread further and more gifts arrived, he was able to support more people. In 1947 he was able to establish a new building called Pingalwara. Today it is described as a centre for hope, health and happiness.

---

1 [*] For more about the story of Puran Singh see: Patwant Singh and Harinder Kaur Sekhon, *Garland Around My Neck: The Story of Puran Singh of Pingalwara* (Birmingham: DTF Publishers, 2001).

Questions to consider:

- Take another look at the image and consider when and how we might demonstrate care for each other.

- Bhagat Puran Singh showed great kindness and cared for the people within his community in India. Who might need kindness, caring and generosity in our community?

Four Star Assembly ✪✪✪✪

The assembly can be extended by discussing acts of kindness. Draw up a table on a flip chart (like the one below) to show how and when people exhibit kindness. Some examples are included but ask the children to make more suggestions.

Who do we give time to?	Who do we give gifts to?	Who do we help to raise money for?	How do we demonstrate kindness in a friendship?
Visiting a sick relative Visiting grandparents Doing voluntary work	Unwanted items to a charity shop Cakes for a cake sale Birthday presents to friends and relatives	Donations to a particular charity School sponsored walk	Through a smile Loyalty Sharing things Doing something together when you may not really want to

Then take the discussions further by considering what practical actions can be taken to support those who need kindness and care in our community.

Five Star Assembly ⭐⭐⭐⭐⭐

Story

There is another story that could be a powerful extension.

It is over 1,200 years old and relates to the Prophet Mohammed when he was living in Mecca. At that time, many people worshipped different idols and Mohammed was working hard to convince them that there was only one true God. However, this did not make him a popular man and some people did not trust him.

Each day as Mohammad walked through the streets he passed the house of an old woman. Out of politeness he always greeted the woman with the traditional, 'Assalam-o-Alaikum', which simply means 'Peace be with you'. Every day when he did this, the woman quickly reached for her sweeping brush and vigorously swept the dust in his direction. This happened day after day for several weeks.

But then one day as he was passing the house he noticed the little old woman wasn't there. He took a few steps past the house and was continuing with his journey when suddenly he stopped and turned back. He needed to know where the woman was and why she hadn't been there to sweep dust in his face!

Mohammed knocked on the door several times. Each time he knocked louder but each time there was no reply. Eventually he decided to open the door and take a look inside. He found the woman slumped in a chair. She was suffering from a fever. He promptly went to fetch help so that she could start to get better. Each day Mohammed visited her until she was feeling well again. He showed her great care and kindness.

Nobody knows what the little old woman thought about her previous behaviour. Maybe she was sorry about sweeping dust into Mohammed's face, but afterwards, each time she was greeted with the words 'Assalam-o-Alaikum' she offered her own friendly greeting and a smile in return.

At the conclusion of this story you could ask the children to consider how it feels when they perform an act of kindness that makes a difference, and also when they receive kindness. They could then compare this with the feelings they have when they decide to be disagreeable or when they have unpleasant things done to them.

43.
Cyberbullying

Three Star Assembly ✪✪✪

Script

In 1943 Ken Olsen, the president of Digital Equipment Corporation, said: 'There is no reason for any individual to have a computer in his home.' In 1943 the chairman of IBM, Thomas Watson, said: 'I think there is a world market for maybe five computers.' Today there are many *individuals* who own five computers! Technology can be used for fabulous purposes, including building lasting friendships. However, it can also cause huge damage. This story is based on the diary of an 11-year-old girl.

Story

It started in the classroom and finished on the Internet. Nadia, who was relatively new to the school, walked into the classroom. Her life had become a misery since the moment she had arrived. There was no sign of her teacher. It was raining outside and it was another wet breaktime. All of a sudden, her school bag was yanked off her shoulder by Katie Gillott. Here we go again, thought Nadia, with tears starting to well in her eyes. She knew what was going to transpire because it had happened a dozen times before. How come there is never

a teacher around when you really need one, she thought. Within seconds her bag was being thrown around by a group of five giggling girls; others just stood around watching. Nadia made vain attempts to catch the bag but she was always that split second too slow. In desperation she shouted out through her tears, 'Please leave me alone!' However, the bag seemed to fly around faster and faster.

Nobody in the class really liked Katie Gillott. They knew she was a bully and they were frightened of her. She was always picking trouble with the other children and trying to belittle them. Some of the others joined in with her out of fear and others simply stood back and observed. They were just glad not to be her target on this occasion.

Just when Nadia thought it couldn't get any worse, one of the girls pulled a mobile phone out of her coat pocket and started filming her frantically running around trying to catch her bag with tears streaming down her face. Eventually she made a last-ditch attempt to catch the bag but fell to the floor sobbing and defeated.

Later that evening Nadia tried to cheer herself up by logging on to her favourite social networking site. She was going to make contact with her pals from her old school. The Internet was wonderful and an escape from the trials of the day. It was as though the Internet was her friend. However, it was now about to turn very cruel. The first thing Nadia saw were photos of her collapsed on the classroom floor in tears. Written alongside was a message saying, 'What a loser!'

Nadia never returned to school the next day, or the one after or ever again. It's a great shame as I think I could have been a friend to her. I look for her and miss her. I feel responsible for what happened because I was one of those who stood by looking on and doing nothing.

Questions to consider:

- What can we do to make sure that anybody new to our school feels safe and secure?

- Which people in the story may have wanted the incident to stop?

- How could any of them have brought about an end to this situation?

- What is the wisest thing to do if you are a victim of any type of bullying?

Four Star Assembly ✪✪✪✪

The end of the story refers to examples of good and bad uses of the Internet. Take a flip chart into assembly and draw up a table like the one below and ask the children to reflect on what they would put in the different columns. Some examples have been included.

Good use of the Internet	Bad use of the Internet
Allows you a wider circle of friends	Reduces face-to-face contact with people
Wonderful source of knowledge	Cyberbullying
Aids learning	Reduces physical activity
Relatively inexpensive	Can lead to sitting in isolation
Develops ICT skills	Could be used to play violent games
Allows you access to music, films and books	

Five Star Assembly ✪✪✪✪✪

Children and young people receive a great deal of guidance about bullying from many sources. However, it can very easily be forgotten in the hurly-burly of school life. Often a powerful saying can provide genuine guidance on how to respond if a cyberbullying incident occurs. For the final part of the assembly, ask the children if they can come up with a short powerful message that captures the idea that the Internet can be used well and badly. A good example could become part of the school rules or guidance about well-being.

44.
Don't Judge a Book by its Cover

Three Star Assembly ⭐⭐⭐

Story

It had reached the point where Ana Vranic was exhausted. She had now been Christmas shopping for several hours. Her bags were getting heavy and her feet were very sore. However, she had now bought most of the things on her list and therefore decided to reward herself with a cup of coffee and a chocolate bar in a cafe.

She had hoped not to have to queue, but the reality was that the restaurant was heaving with people and she knew that probably there were not going to be enough seats. Eventually she got served and struggled with her tray and bags towards the only remaining empty chair. However, she really didn't want to sit in that particular seat because it would mean sharing a table and she didn't like the look of her fellow diner.

Ana looked around in the hope of finding a different table, but there were none, so reluctantly she headed towards the one spare seat. She looked at the young man again. His appearance made her feel very uncomfortable. His face was half concealed by a baseball cap and scruffy hoodie. And she especially didn't like the look of the tattoo she could just glimpse on his neck. However, she had no choice, so she asked if the seat was free and did he mind if she joined him. Slowly he looked up from his mobile phone and, with a blank expression, said, 'Of course, love.'

She was still struggling with her tray and numerous bags but eventually she put the drink on the table and the bags by her feet, and then set off back towards the counter to return her tray mumbling, 'How dare he call me "love"?' as she went. When Ana returned she had the distinct feeling that something was wrong. She looked to check that her bags were still there … yes they were. She checked that her drink was still there … it was. And then she looked to see if her chocolate bar was still there … *it wasn't!* A sense of anger arose within her. How dare he steal her chocolate? But things were about to get a whole lot worse.

As she got to the table, the boy rose from his chair, dropped a chocolate bar wrapper onto the table and said, 'Merry Christmas, Missis.' At that point, Ana Vranic shouted at the top of her voice, 'How dare you!' picked up her coffee and threw it at him! She ran out of the restaurant very upset.

When Ana returned home she didn't even take her coat off – she was so incensed by what had happened. With anger in her voice she started to tell her husband the story of how this awful, scruffy, disgusting youth had stolen her chocolate bar. As she completed her story the tears started to well in her eyes and she began to sob about the terrible events she had just experienced. She reached into her coat pocket to pull out her handkerchief, but instead of that she discovered the chocolate bar she had slipped into her pocket while she had been struggling with her bags and tray in the cafe.

Aghast, she saw an image of the boy with hot coffee dripping down his face. She started to cry once more. Just then the doorbell rang, she looked at her husband and said, 'Will you get that, I'm not in a fit state.' A minute later her husband returned to the room with his arms full and said, 'A young man in a hoodie has just returned your shopping bags!'

Questions to consider:

- Take another look at the boys in the photograph. What words would you use to describe them?

- Then ask this question: What do we really know about any of these boys or their characteristics?

- Who do you consider is the most pleasant character in the story?

- How do you think the boy found out where to return the bags?

- What do you think that Ana should do next?

- What do you think the moral of this story is?

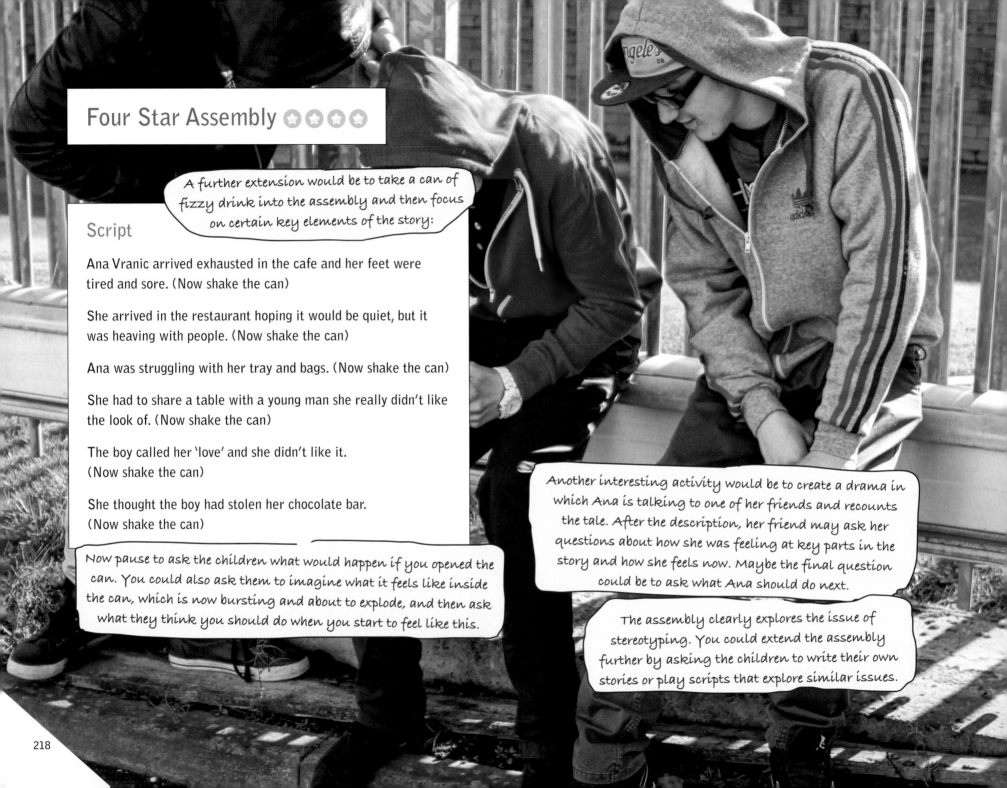

Four Star Assembly ⭐⭐⭐⭐

A further extension would be to take a can of fizzy drink into the assembly and then focus on certain key elements of the story:

Script

Ana Vranic arrived exhausted in the cafe and her feet were tired and sore. (Now shake the can)

She arrived in the restaurant hoping it would be quiet, but it was heaving with people. (Now shake the can)

Ana was struggling with her tray and bags. (Now shake the can)

She had to share a table with a young man she really didn't like the look of. (Now shake the can)

The boy called her 'love' and she didn't like it.
(Now shake the can)

She thought the boy had stolen her chocolate bar.
(Now shake the can)

Now pause to ask the children what would happen if you opened the can. You could also ask them to imagine what it feels like inside the can, which is now bursting and about to explode, and then ask what they think you should do when you start to feel like this.

Another interesting activity would be to create a drama in which Ana is talking to one of her friends and recounts the tale. After the description, her friend may ask her questions about how she was feeling at key parts in the story and how she feels now. Maybe the final question could be to ask what Ana should do next.

The assembly clearly explores the issue of stereotyping. You could extend the assembly further by asking the children to write their own stories or play scripts that explore similar issues.

Five Star Assembly ⭐⭐⭐⭐⭐

If time allows, you could create a follow-up assembly using the tale of Nasreddin's coat or use it for a period of quiet reflection. The story is an Islamic folktale and could therefore also be used to reinforce the key principles of the Islamic faith.

Story

Nasreddin was well respected in his village and popular with everyone around him. One day he was to be the guest of honour at the party of a rich merchant. The problem was that on the day of the party he had forgotten all about it. Instead he went to work in the fields and so he put on his old clothes. Right at the last minute he remembered the party and now he had a dilemma. If he went back to his house to get clean and put on his finest clothes, he knew he would be very late for the party and that would seem awfully rude, so instead he headed straight for the party and didn't bother to get changed.

When he got to the merchant's house nobody would talk to him. In fact they seemed to be ignoring him. And when he sat at the dinner table nobody came to sit with him. Nasreddin felt most uncomfortable and tried to work out why nobody seemed to like him. Feeling very sad, he looked down and remembered he was wearing his dirty old clothes – maybe the people hadn't even recognized him.

As quick as he could, he dashed home and changed into his finest clothes and returned to the banquet where he was suddenly very popular with all those around him. Then Nasreddin took off his coat and started to talk to it. The people looked on as if he was mad because nobody ever talked to a coat. He said to the coat, 'When I came to this party dressed in ragged old clothes nobody liked me and they ignored me. Now that I have come dressed in you, my finest coat, I am suddenly popular, so it is clear that my coat is popular and not me, and so I will leave you here to enjoy the party and come back for you later.'

At that point Nasreddin left the coat and he also left the party.

Acknowledgements

It was nearly seven years ago that I was welcomed into the Independent Thinking family. They are a fabulously talented and diverse group of educationalists who think deeply about schools and education. They also have the amazing capacity to make others think about the needs of our young people. In the course of those seven years I have regularly had the privilege of spending time with them and sharing ideas. Each time this happens I grow as an educationalist. Much of the work I suggest in this book has been shaped by those opportunities and I therefore thank my wonderful colleagues at Independent Thinking. However, I would especially like to thank Dr David George. Just as I was starting to flag, we met up to talk about this book. I spent a truly inspirational and remarkable few hours with him. I thank David for his contributions – I am sure he will recognize his influence on the book.

This book has been truly brought to life by the stunning photographs of Jane Hewitt. These images, in the hands of a skilful teacher, will lead to transformational learning. I first met Jane during the spring of 2013 when she showed me the collection of photographs that now enhance this book. My mind was blown away and I am indebted to her. Please use her pictures with the young people in your school. Used in either the classroom or the assembly hall, they have the capacity to change the world for the better.

About the photographs

Jane Hewitt taught, mainly at secondary level, for 30 years. She still loves learning, discovering new ideas and photography and is rarely found without a camera around her neck.

Jane is a talented photographer, unless where specified all photographs in this book were taken by her.

Many of Jane's images from this book are for sale as postcards or posters for classroom use. See http://www.photoboxgallery.com/ learningthroughalens

Images available on the CD